TO FIGHT
OR
NOT TO FIGHT

TO FIGHT
OR
NOT TO FIGHT

Should a pastor resign under pressure or stay and fight?

By
DR. JEFF J. BARNES

BARNES INSTITUTE
10308 Metcalf Ave. #409
Overland Park, KS 66212-1800

www.barnesinstitute.com

Copyright 2000
Printed in the United States

ISBN: 1-58597-0182

Library of Congress Catalog Card No. 00 090026

Leathers Publishing
4500 College Blvd.
Leawood, KS 66211
1 / 888 / 888-7696

*Affectionately dedicated to my loving wife, Marty,
who twenty-four years ago chose to spend
the rest of her life with me,
and who brings God's grace to me
in ways I never thought possible.
She is my very best friend.*

JEFF J. BARNES is founder and president of Barnes Institute, a ministry to guide pastors and professional leaders in the areas of burnout, stress management, anger management, and forgiveness. Dr. Barnes has served as a pastor, speaker and denominational leader for over twenty-five years. He received degrees from Southwest Baptist University, Southwestern Baptist Theological Seminary, and Midwestern Baptist Theological Seminary. He is the author of *Ten Proven Steps on How to Prevent Burnout*. He and his wife Marty live in Overland Park, Kansas.

Dr. Barnes can be reached for keynote addresses, conferences and seminars at:

Barnes Institute
10308 Metcalf Ave. #409
Overland Park, KS 66212-1800
www.barnesinstitute.com

TABLE OF CONTENTS

Preface

Introduction

Preface

Pastoral ministry, once regarded as a safe and secure vocation, has become in recent years a high-risk undertaking, rivaling business or politics in its hazards to health, longevity and employment security. Churches all over our nation are dealing with internal struggles and are asking their pastors to leave. Recent statistics reveal that every month 1300 pastors are forced to resign or are fired. Forty percent of today's pastors will be out of the ministry within ten years.

When pastors are forced out or resign under fire, they feel lonely and isolated with few resources to sort out what went wrong. I know because I am one that after seventeen years of successful full-time pastoral ministry was forced to resign.

While my wife and I attended a retreat for burned out ministers in Marble Colorado our therapist Dr. Louis McBurney suggested that I write this book. *To Fight or Not to Fight* is not about winning battles or rehashing the wrongs I've suffered at the hands of some church leaders. This book is a survival manual for pastors, as well as a useful guide to congregations whose pastors come under attack by members or groups within the church. It is concerned with the welfare of both pastor and church.

This book provides practical guidelines for the pastor who senses conflict beginning to take place, and gives direction in making a decision to resign or stay and fight. Over the past two and one half years I have interviewed many pastors who have been forced to resign, denominational leaders, and conflict managers. Although following the guidelines in this book are not fool proof and do not guarantee success, they will be helpful in evaluating and determining with God's help what direction to take.

I believe that we pastors need to be better at navigating our way through conflict so we can preserve the love of God in our souls and the call of God on our lives. My prayer for this book is that in some small way, pastors will be encouraged and churches will take a second look at how they can love and support their God given leader.

Introduction

Several years ago in a mid-west town, the deacons and pastor of a local church had an ongoing battle. The deacons decided to take the matter in their own hands and remove the pastor. Their plans were to forcibly remove the pastor at the next Sunday's service by rushing forward just before the message and bodily carrying him out the door.

The pastor received word concerning the plans of his angry deacons, so when Sunday came he was ready. Behind the pulpit he placed a baseball bat and waited for the moment. Sure enough, after the pastoral prayer, three men got up out of the pews and rushed forward to remove the pastor. The pastor saw them coming and reached for his baseball bat. The rest is history. The next day the newspapers reported that after it was all over, ambulances raced to the hospital with three men who were seriously injured. The pastor had won ... or had he?

This true story is an extreme report concerning churches and pastors. Many pastors fantasize about taking matters in their own hands, especially when they feel cornered and no one will stand up for them.

We are living in a day where pastors are becoming an endangered species. Churches all over our nation are having problems; they quickly point the finger at the pastor and make the decision to get rid of him instead of looking at the real issues. Many think that it's much easier to get a new pastor rather than discipline a church member.

Many ministers spend years preparing to serve in a

local church, and are excited about what God can do as they lead a local congregation. Sadly, over a period of time many become disillusioned by the lack of love shown to them and their families. They work long hours, giving their very lives to meet the needs of others. Many ministers are burning out because they continue to give and give and give, but are receiving very little.

When conflict arises, it is normally because of self-will over God's will. All too often God's people break His peace by the sinful and selfish desire for their own wills to rule and reign. Churches today have split. Friends and even families are broken up, and hatred and heartache fill the lives of many believers, all because peace is not ruling in their hearts.

Confrontation is expressed by an attitude of, "Who is in authority here?" The apprehension builds to a critical point and a contest is inescapable. Most pastors are aware of the possible contest of authority and try to avoid it. Many pastors in fear of losing their job give in to the wishes of those exerting the most power, while other pastors try to remain true to the scripture and lead the church.

When a pastor gets into an unavoidable conflict, what should he do? Should he try to keep peace in the church and walk away, exposing himself and his family to the voices of his accusers? Or, should the pastor stay and fight those who believe they are in power, possibly splitting the church? What does the Bible say? These questions and many more will be addressed in this book.

CHAPTER ONE

One Pastor's Story

Seminary Days — An Eye Opener

During my seminary training in the late '70s, I was excited to pastor a small church my last year. I felt fortunate since there were 5,000 students at the seminary and only 300 would ever pastor while in this particular school. My wife and I drove 220 miles each Sunday to pastor 15 people who had been together as a church for over 50 years. I was excited to share from God's Word and lead the people to do evangelism in their local community.

My wife and I learned quickly that the seminary did not prepare me for this particular church. Each Sunday we were passed around to each of the couples to eat Sunday lunch. We found out that we were the entertainment for that specific couple for the day. We enjoyed round one and two, but by round three we began to get drained from hearing the same stories.

I didn't complain about the pay because I was so pleased to become a pastor. The pay had been the same for the past 20 years, $25 a week. On our "trial" Sunday, there was a balance of $25 listed on the front wall as the offering for the day. The next week my wife and I placed our tithe from our secular jobs, which came to the amount of $25; we had actually doubled their income in one Sunday. What happened the next week was despairing for my wife and me. The offering was only $25; we were now paying ourselves!

I worked very hard visiting as many people as I could following the Sunday lunch. Finally, we had one couple accept Christ who wanted to be baptized and join the church. I was thrilled since the church had not had a new member in over 17 years. When I shared my good news with the church, they said, "No, pastor, we don't want any new folk in our midst; why, they will be strangers." You see, I had the naïve idea that as a pastor, all I had to do was rally the saints through preaching and go out leading the church to win the lost to Christ. For the first time in my life I realized that pastoring would be complex.

Mission Church — Doing It Alone

Completing seminary, we became part of a mission church in our home state. We packed up our few pieces of furniture, my books, and our one-week-old son and moved to a new location, ready to begin leading a new group of people. The excitement of pastoring my first full-time church was exhilarating. I could not wait to get to my office each morning and plan a full day of ministry. I would visit as many people as I could who were prospects for the mission church.

Each Sunday, we would see more and more people attend the worship and hear the Word preached. I felt great knowing that God was using me to change lives and give people hope. The church grew quickly, and we began thinking about building an education building.

The first building program that I was in charge of proved to be a valuable experience.

My stamina was unceasing, and I increasingly gathered energy as I ministered to people. In fact, I received energy by doing. I set up tables by myself, rearranged the chairs, wired the sound system, and even filled all of the Lord's supper cups. Interestingly, everyone let me do it and even applauded my energy level. At times, someone would comment, "Wow, I cannot believe all that you get accomplished in a day's time." Statements like that made me work even harder.

The church grew immensely, but it grew predominantly because of my hard work and not by educating the laity. I did a great disservice to the church by not preparing them to use their spiritual gifts to serve God and the church.

The church has had difficulty since I left, especially in the area of finding a pastor with the ability to match my high energy level. I feel a great sadness in my heart for the church because of the way it was born and nurtured; like children who have been taught bad habits and unrealistic expectations, it would battle with lifelong difficulty. I wish that I could go back in time and change what happened. After that experience, empowering people to do ministry became my mode of operation.

Suburban Church — Dealing With Loss

Moving to a new church helped me take what I had learned from past experience and put it into practice. Empowering people to do ministry was my direction from the very beginning, and God provided men and women who had this same vision. The church was in a much larger town with several young couples wanting to make a difference for Christ in the community. They wanted me to lead the way in planning a building program.

The church began to grow rapidly, necessitating a move from the small worship center to the gymnasium until the new buildings were built. The congregation followed with excitement and enthusiasm, resulting in more growth. By the time the builders completed the new buildings, we had grown so much that we had to begin with two worship services.

Immediately following the move into the new worship center, tragedy blew through my life. One morning at 3 a.m. I received a phone call that my father was having a heart attack. My wife and I jumped into our car, beginning the difficult trip to my hometown 70 miles away. On the way to the hospital my mind traveled back 16 years earlier, when my dad had suffered a massive heart attack at 37 years of age. The doctors had said if he ever had another attack he would not survive. I knew that when I arrived at the hospital my 53-year-old father would not be alive.

As I entered the emergency room, I felt as if I was watching myself in slow motion. I went to the room where my father's body was and pulled back the sheet. Stroking his hair, I talked to him and said the things that I had always wanted to say, hoping that God would allow my dad to hear.

Being the first-born of four children, I took responsibility for the funeral arrangements, trying to be the strong one so others could lean on me. The night before the funeral, there were over 500 people who came to the funeral home to try to help us with our great pain. The church where I was pastor ministered to my family and me in a remarkable way. For the first time in my life I sensed what it was like to have people minister to me in a time of need.

The experience of losing my father was a preparation for what was to come in the next four years. One afternoon, I received a phone call that my chairman of deacons' eleven-year-old son had been shot. Immediately rushing to the hospital, I knew something was serious when I saw the life-flight helicopter landing at the emergency room landing zone. I was met by a doctor who asked me to drive the parents to the trauma center 30 miles away as their son was being flown to the hospital. He also asked me to explain to them on the way that their son was brain dead because of the self-inflicted gunshot wound.

The trip to the trauma center was one of the most difficult I have ever made. In just a few hours after we arrived at the hospital, the parents of this 11-year-old boy had to tell their son goodbye. The funeral was the most difficult I have ever performed. I was up until 2 a.m. preparing a message that would bring comfort to a family and friends dealing with a senseless tragedy. God did use me as I simply allowed Him to speak through me.

The next catastrophe took place on an afternoon in the fall. I received a call that my younger brother had been in a three-wheeler accident on our farm. On the way back to my hometown, I envisioned my brother with a broken leg or arm. However, when we arrived at the emergency room, I realized that something was very wrong. My brother's friends were outside the emergency room acting very sad and not talking to us. Opening the door to the same emergency room where my father had died just 15 months earlier, I was met by my brother-in-law. He explained that my brother was killed in a three-wheeler accident.

Again I found myself preparing for a funeral for a family member. My 23-year-old brother was now dead and I had to be the one that others could lean on; at least that's what I thought. I began to bury my feelings so I could continue to work as a pastor and also try my best to help my family survive. I entombed my feelings so well; I could actually preach the Sunday following my brother's death without showing emotion. That day began a journey that would lead to an emotional collapse years later.

Tragedy seemed to encompass my family. The next incident happened while I was serving as a Chaplain of the Army National Guard. Ft. Dix, New Jersey is not a place that holds fond memories for me; my life almost ended there when I was bitten by a tick, which resulted in my contracting Lymes disease. This was at a time when very little was known about the disease. The infection was noticed in such a late stage that I had to be hospitalized and have an IV tube inserted into my arm for ten days, with six million units of penicillin running through my veins every day. One day my heart rate was so low that I almost died. In fact, the pain was so intense that I prayed for God to be merciful and allow me to die. It was over a year before I could function on a normal level as a pastor with heavy demands. I thank God I was in a church that understood and allowed me time to heal instead of discarding me and getting a new pastor.

Following my bout with the Lymes disease, my sister had her leg amputated due to a serious infection. She had been diagnosed from birth as having Spina Bifida, a debilitating disease that led to her amputation. As I dealt with this and many other troubling circumstances, I continued to bury my pain, paint on a contented face, and let people believe that I was strong. In reality, my heart was becoming hardened because I would not allow myself to experience feelings.

Big City Church — Conflict and Change

The next move began the most trying experience of my life. The thought of moving to a larger church helped my ego, even though many warned me that the church was difficult and several previous pastors had been forced to leave because of overwhelming circumstances. I thought, "Others may have faltered, but I can do it." The church was an older traditional church in a growing community. Because of previous difficulty, there were several factions in the church. In prior years, several pastors and staff had been fired or at least forced to leave the church. I should have recognized the pattern, but thought it would be different now.

Beginning at a larger church required a change in my thinking and ministry style. Administration and leadership required an enormous amount of time. The church was in the red financially when I became pastor, but as attention was given to the finances, they started to improve. I found myself spending many hours making sure that everything was running smoothly.

Preaching has always been my strong point, and I realized that preparation took a great amount of time. I knew to get the job done my time had to be structured in the most efficient manner, resulting in many long hours.

Evangelism was strong my first two years. As pastor, I had the privilege of baptizing 100 people per year. The church was excited about the new growth, but the threat of new people caused anxiety and fear to build in some of the long-time members.

Burning the candle at both ends was a challenge; however, I did not realize the toll it would take not only on my body, but also on my mind and emotions. I was one who believed I could do it all, taking pride in getting a great amount of work accomplished in a short amount of time. As I look back on my life, I realize that I allowed myself to accept too many responsibilities, emaciating my energy level.

Evangelism was so important to me that I allowed myself to add an additional ministry serving as a Chaplain and Deputy of the Sheriff's Patrol. The position was a release as I was on the road able to get physically active instead of sitting behind a desk. Death notifications and counseling with the deputies and their families were my major responsibilities. Since I had become accustomed to burying my feelings, it was easy for me to deal with tragedies and make death notifications. Suicides, car accidents, homicides and other tragedies became part of my life. I took satisfaction in the fact that I could view mangled bodies and not become disturbed emotionally; however, at the same time, I was burying the images and feelings deep within me.

Conflict was a daily event. I found myself going from member to member trying to take care of ruptured relationships caused by misunderstandings and friction. I was reminded of the interpretation of the interim pastor who had served before me. He said that the church was "very immature." That phrase came back to haunt me many times, right to the very end.

The height of immaturity was shown during a rehearsal for an annual Easter Pageant. The "angels" were fighting because some of them wanted to be closer to Jesus so they would be seen by the majority of the audience. Another time, some of the mothers of the children in the pageant got into an argument because they wanted more stage time for their aspiring actors. Each year I approached the pageant with great apprehension because, instead of serving as a pastor, my role had diminished to referee.

The stress level became more intense each year. The church was growing numerically, and assimilating new people was difficult, especially as new members began to take leadership roles. This allowed for even more conflict and confrontations concerning the direction of the church. Also, I knew I had several opponents that wanted me gone and were looking for ways to allow that to take place.

Over a period of time the church decided to purchase property and make plans to relocate in the future. The decision began to polarize some of the groups in the church. I knew that the fund-raising process would be difficult and even more stressful. Enough money was raised to purchase the property, but not build buildings. The plan was to pay for the property and then build buildings in phases.

Working on my doctor's degree and serving as vice-president of my state convention was a big mistake. I became over-committed in so many areas, but thought that I would be fine because of the challenges that I had previously overcome in my life. During this same two-year period we hired four more full-time ministers, making the total eight. I was so busy working on my doctorate that I did not do my homework as we called some of the staff, not realizing that some had hidden agendas that were distorted. Two, in particular, wanted to be the senior pastor and were very ambitious.

Physically, I was going downhill. My blood pressure was through the ceiling and I was only getting four hours sleep a night. The work load and stress level was mentally and emotionally draining me. Over-commitment, something that had been a part of my life for years, added to my difficulty.

Six months prior to my decision to leave the church, some of the staff became discontented because I was not spending enough time with them and listening to their needs and hurts. I was away serving on a search committee for our state executive director many days out of each month, and also trying to finish my doctorate.

Without my knowledge, secret meetings began to take place while I was away. Distrust began to breed in the minds of a few staff members, which infected the minds of others over a period of time. One evening, the staff secretly met with two lay leaders from the church and presented a document explaining their distrust of me as a pastor. This document was not brought to my attention until after a Personnel Committee meeting. By the time my wife and I were finally allowed to view the hearsay, several people had already read it and began to believe the accusations. The church leadership held two more meetings without my presence.

As a result of these meetings, I was asked to take a leave of absence so the "situation" could get straightened out. Reluctantly, I agreed to take some time off to relieve some of the stress that I was feeling. Meetings continued to take place, some without my knowledge. I felt helpless as I watched my ministry and character being dissected like a frog in a freshman biology class. During the leave of absence I allowed God to work on my heart and perform surgery on my soul. God revealed to me some areas in my life that needed to be changed in order to be in harmony with Him. Depression and burnout had caused my decisions to be misguided. God had opened my eyes to see that I had become self-sufficient because of my past success. Daily God taught me to lean on Him and not on my own understanding. I was eager to share with the staff what God had been teaching me during my leave of absence. When my wife and I met with the staff, I explained that I was sorry for not spending enough time with them and revealed what God had taught me over the past few weeks concerning my relationship with Him. I was met with silence and skepticism. My heart was crushed as my wife and I left the meeting.

A decision was made to have an outside conflict manager brought in to evaluate and give advice to the church leadership. The consultant interviewed the staff, church leadership, my wife and myself. I was assured that the staff would accept any decision made by the consultant. Two weeks later, he returned with the recommendation that I be allowed time away for healing due to burnout and stress, then I should be restored to the church. I believed this was finally a move in the right direction.

Meeting with the leadership was a frustrating experience for the consultant. He said that his proposal was met with an "ecclesiastical yawn." The staff and some of the church leadership did not want reconciliation, they wanted me gone, believing the problem was beyond the point of no return. Telling my wife the news was one of the most difficult experiences in my life. Realizing that reconciliation was not going to happen, we now had to talk about the possibility of resigning as pastor. We had previously decided that we would not be part of a church split.

There was one more meeting with the church leadership where I had the chance to share my heart and allow them to ask questions. I found myself again with the odds stacked against me. I sat in a room with several angry men who had just had the staff's document leaked to them the night before. Just a few days earlier I was promised by the chairman of personnel that the "alleged document was destroyed and those responsible for the document were reprimanded." I shared what God had been teaching me, asked for their forgiveness, and explained that I could serve them as a better pastor. My declarations were met with disdain from several of the men. Some of them just wanted to berate my ministry over the past eight years. I found out later that since the church had changed so much, some of the "old guard" had been looking for ways to get rid of me for at least three years; now, the staff had handed them the very tool to accomplish their task. Without looking for truth, some of the leadership blindly accepted what was printed. There were some that tried to defend me, but they were treated with repugnance and shut down.

Resignation was what most of the leadership wanted. My wife and I concluded that we must resign or there would be a big fight on the church floor. Many people would be hurt, so we made the decision to walk away rather than allow a confrontation in front of the church. Later, a friend made the observation that, instead of fighting, I had taken a bullet for the church. The graphic image of being shot through the heart exactly conveyed the feeling my family experienced. Sharing my resignation with my teenage children was difficult, causing emotions to flow. My family hugged, prayed and cried together for hours. The next day I was so emotionally drained that I could hardly function, unable to perform even simple tasks. The entire day I sensed I was in a dream, and I kept trying to wake up; then reality would set in, and the sensation of persecution would overpower my mind.

Suicidal thoughts invaded my mind as I worried about how to take care of my family financially. I was at a point in my life where I did not care if I lived or died. In fact, the depression and burnout were so deep, I thought that death would be a welcomed relief. Of course, now I realize these were thoughts from the enemy.

I could not even write my own resignation. My mind could not complete a thought as I tried to write out my final words. The outside conflict manager was gracious enough to write my resignation for me.

God was with us in an extraordinary way. One hour before I was scheduled to resign, God gave my wife and me a boost of strength that would get us through the evening. I made a comment to my wife that God was giving me strength and it was growing inside of me. She said the very same thing was happening to her. That very strength was what guided us through the most difficult task of my career, my resignation.

Driving to the church with my family felt like we were all moving in slow motion. As we entered the church parking lot, we were overwhelmed by all of the cars. Entering the building, we were met by two of the men from the church leadership who ushered us in a room for last-minute preparations. When we walked into the full worship center, an awed silence greeted us. I felt a sensation not unlike the feeling that comes over you as a casket is carried through a crowd of mourners. The meeting began with prayer asking for God's direction. I was asked to share with the congregation as their pastor. I climbed the stairs to the platform where I had previously delivered countless messages from God's Word trying to encourage and lead a flock of people.

I really thought that I would be so emotional that I would be unable to read the entire resignation; however, the boldness God gave me as I surrendered my leadership was very helpful. I spoke with confidence and assurance as I looked into the eyes of the people I loved for the very last time, seeing both bewilderment and compassion. My resignation was as follows:

Dear Church Family,

For the past several months I have been wrestling with several personal and professional matters. I thank you for the past month to work on them full time. Some of the concerns involved my decision to be away from the church working with the state Convention and completing my doctorate studies. Also of concern has been the performance of my ministry to our members in the time of sickness, death and other major crisis. I have also struggled with my ability to lead the staff to be God's best.

All of this has led me to the conclusion that I am exhausted mentally, physically, emotionally and spiritually. Therefore, I am submitting to you my resignation as Senior Pastor.

A major part of my decision is for the well being of the church at this time. Some will feel more positive about this decision than others. However, because of my concern for our church advancing God's kingdom here, I feel this is the best interest of the church body.

I am sure that you will continue to pray for my family as I pray for you. If I have hurt anyone in any way please realize that was not my intention. I do apologize for any distress I have caused you.

I am grateful for the time I will have to be recharged by God as I prepare for God's next assignment. Please remember me at my best. Thanks for the eight years I've had serving as your pastor.

In Christian Love,
Jeff Barnes

Completing the statement, I took my wife by the hand, and with our children following us, we walked down the aisle with the same dependence on God that we had when we were married 21 years earlier. What happened next astonished my family. Applause broke out and people stood to their feet in our honor, sharing with us the appreciation for the eight years of ministering to them and their family members. I feel that we left with dignity and God's leadership. One man expressed the feeling that I left as a gentleman.

Immediately, my family and I began to sense the burden lifting. Even though we did not know what our future would be, God's Word assured us that He would not abandon us. After we left, the church voted to continue our salary for five months so I would have time to heal and find employment elsewhere.

The healing process began as my wife and I attended a retreat for burned-out ministers at the Marble Retreat Center in Marble, Colorado. The retreat center only allows four couples each session, meeting over a period of two weeks for group and individual counseling. I worked through repressed grief over my father and brother's deaths, and over the wounds of other events which had caused pain in my life. The two weeks proved to be the beginning of a new direction that God had planned for our lives. Worshipping God in the majestic mountains validated His love for us as we worked through difficult moments from our past. I learned that I have a problem stuffing my emotions deep inside of me and allowing others to cause pain without expressing my true feelings. Changes are taking place as I now attempt to share the truth and my emotions in love and kindness.

The healing process is a course that must be intentional. We have spent two years in therapy as we have worked on our marriage, our parenting skills, and our relationship with God.

CHAPTER TWO

Pastoral Termination — The Effects

Forced Termination — The Epidemic

John Maxwell, the founder of the Injoy Life Club, states that every month 1,300 pastors are forced to resign or are fired. Nearly 30 percent have been terminated at least once. He further states that in a decade, 40 percent of today's pastors will be in another line of work. Every day, 75 percent of churches are hindered because of conflict between the pastor and people or between the church members.[1] The problem of forced terminations is truly an epidemic that is damaging the cause of Christ in our nation.

According to a survey conducted by the Pastoral Ministries department of Focus on the Family, 45 percent of pastors suffer from burnout. Ninety-five percent of pastors struggle with discouragement. Eighty percent believe the pastoral ministry has effected their families negatively.[2] Pastors are leaving the ministry at an alarming rate; it is time to say enough is enough.

Forced Termination — The Definition

A forced termination is when a pastor does not choose to leave the church, but feels he must leave because of the pressure placed on him by the leadership of the church. Sometimes the pressure placed on the pastor is informal; a group of leaders from the church requests the pastor resign "without making a fuss." Other times the church board passes a resolution terminating the pastor and removes the pastor's salary from the church budget.

It does not matter what type of church government system is within the church: Protestant, Catholic, or Jewish; or presbyterial, congregational, or episcopal; involuntary terminations happen. The pastor may finally make a decision to resign to keep dissension from happening in the church. Whether the decision to "let the pastor go" is made by a Bishop or voted by an entire congregation, the results are still the same; there is a devastating effect on the pastor and his family.

Forced Termination — The Phases of Grief

Being forced to leave a church is like dealing with death. Several years ago Elizabeth Kubler-Ross in her book *On Death and Dying*[3] opened the thinking of many to understanding the stages of grief. Many pastors who have been forced to leave their ministry area have experienced similar stages of grief.

The first stage is denial. Many pastors express the thought that "this cannot really be happening to me. I have given my life for this congregation, why are they turning on me and wanting me to leave?" Denial really functions as a buffer after difficult news.

When the first stage of denial cannot be maintained any longer and reality begins to set in, the pastor begins to realize that "this is really happening to me, this is not a mistake or a dream." Feelings of anger begin to sneak in. The logical question becomes, "Why me?" The pastor begins to think of the long hours spent in sermon preparation, counseling, administration, and committee meetings. He begins to feel the anger grow inside of him, but cannot express it because a pastor is to be one that does not let his anger out. He must be in control at all times.

Bargaining is another stage the pastor experiences through the forced termination. He bargains with God, and maybe even the leadership of the church that is trying to force him to leave. The pastor begins to try to comply with the demands of the board members who want him to meet certain expectations concerning their concepts of pastoring. The more he tries to meet their conditions, the more they require.

When the minister realizes that he must resign or be fired, a stage of depression sets in. Like a terminally ill patient who has had all of the surgeries and tried all the possible treatments, his bargaining is replaced with a sense of great loss. The minister who has exhausted all of the possibilities for negotiation begins to think through all of the fears that are rushing through his mind. The fear of not being able to support his family leads to depression and anxiety. "What about my future?" and "Will I be able to pastor again?" are questions that consume the minister's thinking. Many times, the minister who is forced to resign is worried about seeing people from the church he pastored and senses uneasiness when he does encounter them.

Depression is a stage that the pastor and his family can stay in for a long time unless determined steps are taken to accept the termination and move on with life.

Ministers who have been forced to terminate may need counseling, leading them to the final stage, acceptance. When a minister accepts what has happened to him, he then has the ability to make constructive decisions about his future.

As the minister regroups, he can then look at himself and determine where he made mistakes that might have contributed to the need for forced termination. Looking inside can be difficult and painful, but is necessary to make sure that the same mistakes will not be made again.

Forced Termination — The Difficulties

There are times that pastors are simply at the mercy of congregational whims. Sadly, many pastors are blindsided by a few strong-willed, self-appointed congregational magistrates. In these cases, many churches relinquish their collective responsibility to discipline the domineering members, leaving the pastor to defend himself.

As one pastor who quit the ministry explained, pastors are like athletic coaches. A coach must produce annual winning teams or he will be "booted" by protesting alumni. Like coaches, pastors very seldom have someone to defend him or her when they are forced to quit their position. By contrast, in almost any other field of employment there is built-in protection. DeWitt Matthews in his book *Capers of the Clergy*[4] says: "School teachers and educational administrators, if threatened with discharge, are protected from mistreatment by strong organizations that supply topflight lawyers to plead their cases."

Pastors forced to resign have a difficult time finding a position in another church. Many pulpit committees will push the pastor's resume to the back of the pile and back off from further investigation if the pastor is "in between" churches. By contrast, in almost any other profession a desire for change and a move to a different position is considered normal. A mechanic unhappy with his employer can simply take another job across the street, even with more pay, and is normally not frowned upon.

In the secular world, when a person leaves one position and simply wants a change of scenery and a new challenge, he does not have to fear censure. However, a pastor fears being blackballed by other churches when he leaves a church without another position to go to. The average church member does not understand the dilemma their pastor faces when forced to resign. Their mind is in the secular world rather than the "church world."

Most of this dilemma concerning pastoral tenure and forced termination is a result of denominations not seeing this problem as a major concern. It is time that denominational leaders begin looking for ways to educate our churches concerning the epidemic of our pastors leaving the ministry.

In the meantime, pastors all over our nation are dealing with grief over their calling, as the worry lines deepen on their wives' faces, and their children weep behind closed doors. It is dishonorable, immoral, and disgraceful for pastors all over this land to feel compelled to end their ministries while very little is being done about the irresponsible system of pastoral tenure. Leaders in advisory capacities are responsible before God to lead out in resolving this complex predicament.

END NOTES

1 Maxwell, John, *Relationships, A New Beginning or a Bitter End,* Enjoy Life Club Tape Series Vol. 12 No. 10 - April 1997.

2 Dobson, Shirley, *Ministering to the Minister,* Christian American, Vol. 8 Num. 5.

3 Kubler-Ross, Elizabeth, *On Death and Dying,* (New York: MacMillan Publishing Co., 1969).

4 Matthews, DeWitt, *Capers of the Clergy, The Human Side of the Ministry,* (Grand Rapids:Baker Book House, 1976), 95-96.

CHAPTER THREE

Forced Termination — The Causes

In Acts 27, the Apostle Paul describes his famous storm experience on his voyage to Rome. *"We took such a violent battering from the storm that the next day they began to throw the cargo overboard. On the third day, they threw the ship's tackle overboard ..."* Later, as the battering continued, Paul spoke to the distressed passengers and crew, saying, *"I urge you to keep up your courage, because not one of you will be lost; only the ship will be destroyed."*

Notice that in the storm the crew threw the baggage over to save the men. Interestingly, when conflict arises in many churches, the cry will come like a storm blowing, "Throw the pastor overboard, we must save the ship!" In some cases, the church leadership wants to protect the years of baggage, refusing to examine their deteriorated condition.

Many churches have a history of forcing their pastors to resign. My last pastorate was one that had asked the two previous pastors to resign. I was the third in a few years forced to leave the congregation.

Until churches begin to look at their history, pastors will be forced to walk the plank into the waters of incertitude. When pastors are dependent on the institutions for their protection and status, most of them will drown under the pressure.

A Chronic Problem

Your Church magazine did a special report concerning the problem of forced terminations in the ministry. Nine out of ten pastors (91%) know three to four others who have been forced out of pastoral positions. In fact, one-third of all pastors (34%) serve congregations who either fired the previous minister or actively forced his or her resignation. Perhaps more telling, nearly one-fourth (23%) of all current pastors have been forced out at some point in their ministry.

In 1996, Your Church mailed 999 surveys to a random selection of U.S. pastors who subscribe to *Leadership, Christianity Today*, and *Your Church*. A total of 593 pastors responded, giving 59 percent response rate. Here are the survey results:

Reasons for Forced Exit
Conflicting visions for the church 46%
Personality conflict with board member(s)......... 38%
Unrealistic expectations 32%
Lack of clear expectations................................. 24%
Personality conflicts (not with board members). 22%
Theological differences....................................... 21%
Personality conflict with Senior Pastor 19%

Forced Exit vs. Termination
Of those forced out:
Terminated 13%
Forced to resign 58%

Pressured to resign 29%

During Which Pastorate Do Terminations Occur?
First 29%
Second 43%
Third 24%
Fourth 11%
Fifth 12%
Sixth... 4%

Driving Forces Behind Pastor's Exit
Small faction of congregation 43%
Board member(s) 32%
Own convictions 22%
Senior pastor 18%
Denominational supervisor 14%
Staff member(s)... 5%
Large portion of congregation 4%

Percentage of High Risk
"Some churches can be a toxic environment for pastors and their careers. The majority of ousted pastors (62%) were forced out by a church that had already forced out one or more pastors in the past. At least 15% of all U.S. churches fall into this category, having forced out two or more pastors. On average, these churches have forced out three to four pastors."

Churches Dismissing More than One Pastor
2 pastors 27%
3 pastors 33%
4 pastors 14%

5 pastors 11%
6-7 pastors 11%
8 or more pastors... 4%

Time it takes to find another pastoral position:
3 months or less 45%
4-6 months 18%
7-9 months 8%
10-12 months 8%
13-15 months 5%
Over 15 months 16%

I received a survey from the Southern Baptist Convention Sunday School Board where a survey was conducted by associations asking the number of pastors who experienced forced termination in their ministry area in 1996. The total was 1,089. The second questions was; "In your experience, what are the most common causes of forced termination?" Here are the top five results:

1. Control issues — who's going to run the church.
2. Poor people skills on part of the pastor.
3. Church's resistance to change.
4. Pastor's leadership style — too strong.
5. Church was already conflicted when the pastor arrived.

In my research and experience, I have found that some common trends occur when pastors are terminated. Some problems occur because of the pastor, and others because of the church.

Over-committed Pastors

Because of their nature and calling, pastors have a tendency to accept too many responsibilities. No matter how much energy a pastor possesses, trying to do too much will cause him to fall short in the eyes of the congregation.

Pastoring is one of the only professions where each member has their own personal job description for the minister to fulfill. Some members believe that visitation is to be a priority, while others believe that counseling is the vital role. The duty of preaching may be a high expectation for some, while administration is the priority for others. If a pastor tries to keep everyone happy, he will be over-committed and open himself to criticism by all.

The following is an anecdote that I share at Pastors' Conferences that gets several laughs but stings with the reality of the obvious:

CHAIN LETTER: TO GET A PERFECT PASTOR

The results of a computerized survey of the expectations of church members now indicate the following characteristics of a perfect pastor:

- *He preaches exactly 15 minutes, but includes all that the Bible has to say about the sermon subject.*

- *He condemns everyone else's sin except yours, and never says anything that anyone might disagree with.*

- *He works from six a.m. until midnight, but gets eight hours of sleep to stay healthy.*

- *He prepares three sermons a week for 40 years and never repeats an idea, illustration or joke.*

- *He makes $250 a week, wears good clothes, buys good books, drives a new car, plus gives $100 a week to the poor.*

- *He is 28 years old and has been in the ministry for 30 years.*

- *Half of his hair is youthful blonde, and the other side is gray to give him that distinguished look.*

- *He has a burning desire to work with teenagers and spends all of his time with senior adults.*

- *He's a close personal friend to every member.*

- *The perfect pastor smiles all of the time with a straight face because he has a sense of humor that keeps him seriously dedicated to his work.*

- *He makes 15 visits a day to church families, homebound, and hospitalized while he spends all of his time evangelizing the unchurched, and he is always in his office when you need him.*

- *He has four kids who never get into trouble, a wife who cooks like Betty Crocker, councils like Joyce Brothers, prays like Hanna, and looks like Marilyn Monroe, without making anyone jealous.*

If your pastor does not measure up to these expectations, simply send this chain letter to other churches whose pastors fail to meet these reasonable standards. Then, bundle up your pastor and send him to the church at the top of the list. In one year you will receive 1,643 pastors — and one of them should be perfect.

Warning! Keep this letter going, one church broke the chain and got its old pastor back.

It is impossible for a pastor to fulfill every expectation that church members place on him. When he tries, the outcome will always be an impasse between the pastor and the leadership of the church.

Speed Leas from the Alban Institute explains that many pastors and staff don't have objective standards by which to assess their progress or success.[1] Finding completion is a difficulty in the ministry; there are always other members you can visit, more counseling that needs to be done, sermons that need to be written, and calls that need to be made. Because of this, some pastors need encouragement from different members and leadership in order to feel successful.

The pastor must understand his capacity for autonomy, or the inner ability to govern himself. The successful pastor will have the capacity to balance and resolve opposing demands not only within himself, but also between himself and his congregation.[2]

Ultimately, the pastor must look to God and His Word for direction and encouragement. Security only comes through the minister's relationship with God, not in trying to please all the people, which is a hopeless task.

In Jesus' parable of the talents, it was the poor servant who failed to take the initiative, to assert his own
judgment, and to use what was given to him in advance.
The servant who invested his talents wisely was the one
commended by our Lord. Consequently, when we use our
time properly, investing our lives in the areas God has
designed, we have a greater sense of completion.

As the pastor focuses on the ministry areas in which
God has gifted him, he will find excitement and fulfill-
ment. Learning to say "no" to other responsibilities is difficult, but needed if the pastor is to remain sharp in the
ministry. Empowering the laity to do ministry is time-
consuming; however, this preparation is a must if the
church is going to move forward for the cause of Christ.

Pastors Experiencing Burnout

Burnout is the gradual process by which a person in
response to prolonged stress; physical, mental and emotional strain detaches from work and other meaningful
relationships.

Most people who are in burnout are in total denial of
the problem. The gradual process of prolonged stress,
long hours, dealing with difficult people and lack of rest
finally take its toll.

Sixty-five percent of all adults in North America suffer from some type of stress on a weekly basis. Each year
320 billion dollars are spent in medical costs and lost
productivity because of stress.

Ministers are not protected from burnout. In the professional realm it takes on the form of exhaustion which
causes us to stop growing spiritually. When we stop growing, we are in trouble.

When the minister is effected by burnout, he feels depressed. Depression is a normal part of living. But the minister is not supposed to be depressed. He is to help others deal with their depression. It is not only shocking to his church members when they find their minister is fighting depression, it is shocking to the minister himself.

Symptoms of Approaching Burnout

One of the hobbies that I enjoy the most is flying. I love the feeling of being in the air gliding like a bird. The one thing that I depend on to stay in the air are the gauges on the dashboard. My airspeed gauge reveals how fast I am flying. As a pilot, I know what the manufacturer's limits are concerning the speed. If I go beyond the limit the airplane will crash. I must also pay attention to the altimeter, the artificial horizon, the turn and bank, as well as the airspeed gauge. I am constantly scanning the gauges as I fly to my desired destination.

A Loran is one of my most trusted friends. It tells me what direction to fly to get to my ultimate destination. If I stray from the direct path, the Loran will warn me and even tell me how to correct my path. Without paying attention to my gauges, I would surely be lost and eventually crash.

The same is true with life. I am convinced that we all have gauges that keep us on proper healthy paths for life. If we stray, one or more of the gauges will warn us.

The Four Gauges in Life that will Detect Burnout
1. Our *Physical* Gauge.

One of the first areas that we sense burnout is physically. We feel tired all the time. Exhaustion is nothing to be ashamed of; it is the body telling us what we need to know. When we get to our limit physically, our body will speak to us.

Physical Symptoms
- **Dizziness**
- **Backaches**
- **Weakness**
- **Headaches**
- **Chest pains**
- **Heartburn**
- **Frequent urination**
- **Accident proneness**
- **High blood pressure**
- **Dry mouth or throat**
- **Neck pain**
- **Constipation**
- **Indigestion**
- **Stomach pains**
- **Diarrhea**

If you are experiencing several of the physical symptoms of burnout, you need to see your doctor. Below are some serious danger signs that will help you determine if you are in burnout. Each danger sign will be dealt with in more detail.

Physical Danger Signs
➤ **Exhaustion and Fatigue**
➤ **Becoming Less Active**
➤ **Change of Work Style**
➤ **Sleep Deprivation**

➤ **Dependency on Stimulants**
➤ **Weight Loss or Gain**
➤ **Sexual Dysfunction**
➤ **Psychosomatic Complaints**

➤ *Exhaustion and Fatigue*

Maybe you are still holding it together at work. Still, can you relate to this sequence? As soon as you arrive home from the office, you head for the kitchen, grab a bag of chips and a soda, turn on the tube, collapse in your favorite recliner and you're comatose for the rest of the evening.

Lack of energy associated with feelings of tiredness and trouble keeping up with one's usual routine of activities is the first warning sign of burnout. Burnout will show up in your body long before you realize or accept the fact that things are out of control. You begin to realize that your body does not work like it should. You find yourself comparing your life to earlier years. When the alarm goes off, you cannot pop out of bed like in earlier days. Your energy level does not last all day long.

A long-term exposure to stress and burnout can create problems with our bodies. Studies have shown that heart disease is linked to cholesterol levels, which increase with stress. We know that alcohol consumption, obesity, smoking, high salt intake and heredity can all raise blood pressure; but now we also know that stress and burnout can be a major factor in triggering the onset of hypertension.

Some of the diseases that are being blamed to long-term burnout are coronary heart disease, hypertension, kidney disease, and arteriosclerosis.

➤ Becoming Less Active

When you experience burnout, activities are nerve-racking. It's difficult to keep your attention span centered for any length of time. You find it's difficult to relax while doing some things that you used to enjoy.

The consequences are that you do more and more with less and less satisfaction. You do not sense the gratification that you once did.

The pattern of exercise is hard to get into. You find more excuses not to exercise than you find reasons to exercise. There is very little enthusiasm.

When the enthusiasm is not present it's very difficult to get excited about doing anything that was previously bringing satisfaction.

Usually burnout victims are people who have been able to do things quickly. However, as burnout takes place, your own ability to accomplish things diminishes. Impatience and irritability increases toward others.

➤ Change of Work Style

When a person goes through burnout there is a drastic difference in what is being accomplished at work. In many cases the victim of burnout will withdraw from decisive leadership and work habits. Or, on the other hand, they will become more and more demanding, inflexible, or tyrannical, which only causes the cycle of burnout to worsen.

Burnout victims experience complex feelings of bitterness, anger, and resentment because they are not being appreciated for their work. When burnout has taken a long-term hold, it is a small step from feeling unappreciated to feeling mistreated or threatened. Calling in sick or compounded absenteeism is a true sign that the worker is in a burnout stage.

Just about any work situation can be a potential source of stress and difficulty. The way we perceive our work situation will determine the stress level and whether or not we are burned out. The following are common job related stress factors that can lead to burnout on the job. Keep in mind that stress and burnout are different. Burnout is the result of prolonged stress in a person's life.

- **Feeling overwhelmed by the work**
- **Feeling of boredom**
- **Inability to meet deadlines**
- **Poor time management**
- **Conflict with supervisors**
- **Conflict with colleagues**
- **Unable to adapt to change**

➤ *Sleep Deprivation*

Each of us needs a particular number of hours of sleep in order to function at peak capacity. When we do not get enough sleep because of life's demands we can experience a sleep disorder. When a person is in burnout they normally are sleep deprived.

Many who experience burnout have an attitude that they can sacrifice sleep in favor of long work hours. Sleep deprivation can add to the burnout by causing daytime sleepiness, irritability, a reduction of decision-making skills, a reduced ability to concentrate, and adverse effects on physical health.

Doctors tell us that lack of sleep causes a decline in our immune system. Normal sleep changes the activity of the immune system. Certain types of blood cells fight infection and ward off disease. After we fall asleep, these cells rapidly decrease in the blood. Many doctors believe that these cells move from the bloodstream into the tissues to clean out any bacterial invaders. When we are ill, we normally want to crawl into bed. Being tired while ill may be our body telling us that sleep will help our immune system help us get better.

➤ *Dependency on Stimulants*

For many in burnout they begin to change their lifestyle. One example is moving from one or two cups of coffee to eight, ten and twelve cups of coffee because the energy level is not there like it used to be. More and more sugar and caffeine is taken in.

Mild sedatives are now taken because of the sleep deprivation. Although sedatives can be used effectively for a period of time, they can be habit-forming, even those purchased over-the-counter. Many in burnout manifest a psychological dependence on sedatives.

Regular use of sedatives over a long period of time can result in tolerance, which means that the body becomes accustomed to them. Larger and larger doses are needed to get the same effect.

Alcohol addiction is another common occurrence when a person reaches the burnout stage. The burnout victim uses alcohol; to relieve anxiety, to avoid responsibility, to avoid unresolved conflict in family relationships, and to dull the sense of low self-esteem.

➤ *Weight Loss or Gain*

A certain amount of weight gain is normal. But a person who continues to gain weight has a more serious problem than the normal gaining of a few pounds.

Eating more and finding excuses to eat snacks between meals and feeling the need to snack as you watch television is a sign of approaching burnout.

Just as serious as gaining weight is the problem of losing weight at the rate of inordinate or unplanned stages. Not having an appetite, or finding excuses for not eating balanced meals is another sign of approaching burnout.

➤ Sexual Dysfunction

One of the leading causes of sexual problems is stress, which is the forerunner to burnout. Failure to recognize stress and burnout as a cause of sexual dysfunction can lead to serious emotional disorders and permanent loss of sexual desire.

In the male, the sex hormone can be critically inhibited as a result of burnout. Therefore, not only is the sex drive lowered, stress from the sexual dysfunction can spiral into a vicious cycle that gets worse over time. Couples begin to find ways to avoid intimacy in order to avoid stress.

Sexual problems in themselves are an immense cause of stress. Becoming impotent or frigid can easily lead to depression. Many good marriages have broken up because couples did not realize that one partner or both were experiencing burnout.

Here's a specific example:

John becomes aggravated at some of the things his deacons say to him. Since he needs the job, he cannot do much about the difficulty of the fear of losing his job.

Every time he has a dispute with the deacons, John has a stress reaction. The reactions over a period of time come more easily and are of a longer duration with each encounter. Eventually, the mere expectation of a confrontation will bring about a stress reaction. Just by thinking about his deacons, John experiences stress reactions at home, even while trying to have times of intimacy with his wife.

If there's one action we can take, it's to include our spouse or be included by our spouse in order to gain the strength needed to overcome a problem that usually cannot be dealt with alone.

➤ *Psychosomatic Complaints*

A person experiencing burnout will have more complaints of headaches, colds, backaches and similar ailments. Physical ailments seem more conventional and much easier to accept than emotional ailments. Physical symptoms are many times prolonged by the burnout victim's emotional stress.

When a person is going through burnout there are normally more physical complaints made than usual. When the victim uses the physical problems as "scapegoats" for problems encountered, he denies that he is in burnout.

2. Our *Emotional* Gauge

Many professional psychologists believe that what we think controls how we feel. When a person experiences burnout he is prompting unpleasant thoughts which lead to unpleasant feelings. If a victim of burnout thinks, "I wonder why people don't accept or like me," they will feel vulnerable or even fearful. Here are a few danger signs of how we are effected emotionally when experiencing burnout.

Emotional Danger Signs
➤ *Fearfulness*
➤ *Depression*
➤ *Withdrawal*
➤ *Irritability*
➤ *Vulnerability*
➤ *Emotional Difficulty*
➤ *Anxiety*
➤ *Anger*

➤ *Fearfulness*

When a person is in burnout, they are fearful of so many things. Many fear losing their job, their families, their home, and even their identity. Here's the best definition of fear:

False
Evidence
Appearing
Real

There are basically three dominant fears, beyond the fear of death:

- **Fear of Rejection**, which is the fear of being made a fool or failure in the company of others.
- **Fear of Change**, which is moving into unknown areas, sacrificing external securities.
- **Fear of Success**, which is an expression of guilt associated with our desire for self-gratification.

Fear of rejection can be traced to criticisms that we heard from our parents, our teachers, as well as our peers. If we were told as a child "you will never amount to anything", the fear of rejection is always in our minds. We must learn to tell ourselves that is false evidence appearing real.

The fear of change is in the mind of the burnout victim because he is afraid the security system of the job, home, health, and family may change.

The fear of success is really the fear of trying. The burnout victim says, "I cannot imagine myself successful. I can see it for others, but I cannot see it for me."

➤ *Depression*

Depression affects everyone in different ways at different times. Most people feel down or "blue" now and then. Many people have more serious periods of depression, but are still able to meet daily responsibilities. Some people become so severely depressed that they can't face the problems of daily living. They may abuse alcohol and/or drugs or become suicidal.

There are many ways to classify depression. One simple and useful method is by degree of severity.

Mild Depression
- Significant events such as holidays, anniversaries, a new job, a move, as well as boredom and frustration can produce a temporary "down" mood.
- Postpartum depression (after giving birth) is a common type of mild depression. However, it can become severe if not dealt with over a period of time.
Treatment is usually not needed. A change of situa-

*tion, pace, etc. is usually enough to brighten up a "blue"
mood.*

Moderate Depression

Symptoms are similar to those of mild depression,
but more intense and longer lasting.

- **An unhappy event** such as loss of a loved one, career setback, etc., is usually the cause. A person is
  aware of unhappy feelings, but can't always stop
  them.
- **Daily activities** may be harder (but usually still
  possible) to cope with.
- **Suicide** may be a danger. It may seem like the only
  "solution" as pain gets worse.
  Professional help may be necessary.

Severe Depression

Loss of interest in the outside world and serious prolonged behavior changes are characteristic.

- **Deep inner imbalances** are usually the cause. Sometimes another disorder such as schizophrenia, alcoholism or drug addiction may be related to depression.
- **Physical symptoms** often become obvious. The person may suffer from delusions that his or her body is
  changing.
- **Manic-depressive illness** is a form of depression in
  which the person goes from extreme highs to deep lows.
  Professional treatment is necessary.

Victims of burnout are also dealing with depression.
Untreated depression can disrupt work, family relations
and social life. But depression can be treated successfully.

In many burnout cases the working environment can cause depression as well as serious interpersonal conflicts, loss of a loved one, unfavorable family relationships, etc.

Psychotherapy and medication are often used in treating moderate and severe depression. Medication like antidepressants to correct shortages or imbalances of certain chemicals in the brain can sometimes bring relief in three to four weeks. Psychotherapy helps many depressed people become more self-aware and better able to cope with their problems. Treatment methods include individual counseling, group therapy, psychoanalysis, etc. Whatever the method, the goal of treatment is to overcome depression by providing support and help, examining the underlying causes of depression, working out possible solutions to problems, etc. Seriously depressed people should avoid amateur "therapy" from friends and family.

➤ *Withdrawal*

People on the edge of burnout have less time and energy for relationships since more and more time and effort is concentrated on just "keeping up." The victim of burnout begins to detach and withdraw from people with whom he had a close relationship. The withdrawal may be missing a weekly lunch appointment to complete avoidance of a close work-mate or friend. The burnout victim begins to question the value of friendship and activities — even of life itself.

➤ *Irritability*

Normally, burnout victims are people who have been

able to handle things and even accomplish tasks quickly. However, as burnout takes over, their own ability to accomplish things decreases, and their impatience grows and causes problems with others. They are irritated with and blame co-workers and family for things that were their own fault more than the fault of others.

Over a period of time the burnout victim experiences complex feelings of bitterness and resentment because they are not being appreciated for their added efforts. In reality the burnout victim may be generating reduced results. Rather than acknowledging that, they blame others for their diminished results.

➤ *Vulnerability*

When a person faces burnout they are vulnerable. Their behavior changes as they find themselves doing things that their normal character would never allow. Many burnout victims find themselves having an extramarital affair, getting involved in pornography, turning to alcohol, etc. just to find some type of escape.

➤ *Anger*

Anger is a normal human feeling that everyone experiences. The key question concerning anger is how do you deal with it? With most burnout victims they deny their anger. When anger is denied and turned inward the result is depression. I will discuss how to deal with anger in chapter ten.

3. Our *Mental* Gauge

Burnout shows up mentally in the form of feelings of failure as a person. For men, it is especially seen in the workplace. Most men get their self-esteem from their work. When burnout hits, many men begin to think that they are not as productive or effective as they used to be. Signs of cynicism, negativism, and increased irritability become commonplace. Burnout victims may feel hopeless and frustrated by a sense of helplessness, self-doubt, or hopelessness, which can lead to depression.

Mental Danger Signs
➤ *Disorientation*
➤ *Suspicion*
➤ *Poor Judgement*
➤ *Irrational Guilt*
➤ *Suicidal Thoughts*

➤ *Disorientation*
As burnout continues, the victim will have increased difficulty with his thought process. His thoughts will begin to wander and his concentration spans will become increasingly limited. The ability to remember appointments, dates, and even names will become commonplace. Speech patterns will falter and the burnout victim may even forget what he was going to say next, leaving a long pause between thought processes.

Some burnout victims may joke about their disorientation by referring to increased age or senility. Deep on the inside the burnout victim will have increased agitation and inward stress because of the disorientation.

➤ *Suspicion*
When a person goes through burnout, his perspective is changed. Before, he could see things from a broad

context. Now he has tunnel vision, seeing only a small part of the picture. He feels more "on trial" than before. When someone pays him a compliment, the burnout victim becomes suspicious. "I wonder what he meant by that?" he laments when he is affirmed about something. Clinically, what I am talking about is paranoia. The feeling is painful no matter what the label is. It is best to deal with suspicion before it becomes paranoia.

The main problem of being suspicious is the draining effect that keeps us on alert and defensive all of the time. The suspicious person uses all of his energy protecting himself. Therefore, there is very little spontaneity in life like laughing, crying, playing, or enjoying life.

The suspicious person never feels like he "starts" anything. It is always someone else that has a problem. So, many burnout victims experience problems in their personal relationships. Over periods of time people begin to "shun" them. Very few people want to be with a person that does not trust them. Friends get farther and farther away from them.

➤ Poor Judgement

Self-defeating behavior is truly a sign of burnout. The burnout victim does not act like he used to. He begins to look for ways to relieve the mental, emotional, and even physical pain he is experiencing. Behavioral symptoms of burnout include abuse of chemicals, spending less time at work, exhibiting tardiness and absenteeism, impersonal and stereotyped communications, etc.

Many burnout victims are forced to terminate their position at work, or are fired. This adds to the problems that the burnout victim is already experiencing. Life can become like a downward spiral if the victim does not get help. Burnout victims not only make poor judgements at work, but also at home. Marriages tend to become troubled with the burnout victim. Using poor judgement will effect the marriage in a negative manner. Sad, but many burnout victims can end up divorcing.

➤ *Irrational Guilt*

Burnout victims have the feeling that they are getting a raw deal because of who and what they are. It is much easier to be down on yourself than to be up on yourself. It is easier because other people accept it more easily. One of the chief causes of irrational guilt is the "ought to" trips we permit people to put on us. We permit them to occur because we develop some kind of obligation to these persons. When the burnout victim tries to please everyone, he loses his identity. We must understand that we are unique. We will never please everyone, no matter how hard we try. In fact, if we allow others to change who we are, we will still never please them and they will resent us even more.

➤ *Suicidal Thoughts*

Just as burnout, rather than being a form of stress, is really the end result of unrelieved stress, suicide is the result of other factors. It is important to look at suicidal behavior as a symptom of something deeper rather than the cause itself.

Interviews with suicidal patients show that many had bouts with depression shortly before their suicide attempts and felt a sense of hopelessness and futility in dealing with life situations.

Warning Signs of Suicide:
- A significant loss — death of a spouse, loss of a job, etc.
- Severe health problems
- Intense emotional pain, depression
- Intense feelings of hopelessness
- An intense need to achieve
- Chronic self-destructive behavior — alcoholism, drug abuse, eating disorder, etc.

A common misconception involves the fear that to mention suicide to a depressed person will bring about the thoughts that have not occurred previously. Truthfully, to lovingly confront a person with a question about suicidal thoughts can be the first step toward reversing suicidal thinking.

4. Our *Spiritual* Gauge.

Spiritual symptoms of burnout include doubt concerning one's value system or beliefs; drawing conclusions that a major change is necessary such as divorce, a new job, or relocation. People can become angry or bitter at God and withdraw from fellowship.

When a burnout victim is spiritually exhausted they seem to have lost perspective and have failed to recognize their own limits. They normally experience a gradual increased feeling that God is powerless and that they themselves are the only ones with power to help in their prevailing situation. They refuse either consciously or unconsciously to depend on God's power and try to play God themselves. Over a period of time the burned out victim feels like giving up, believing that others, including God, have given up on them.

Burnout is serious, but for those who are feeling its effects, there is hope.

Expectation vs. Reality

Burnout involves unfulfilled expectations; being worn out because what one thought would happen has not. Unfulfilled expectations relate many times to rewards that were expected, but not received, rewards such as: a sense of satisfaction or completeness, happiness, praise, or a sense of security.

There is, of course, no such thing as a perfect job. Whatever career we choose, there will always be the problem of adjusting our expectations to meet reality. This often happens when we begin pastoring, or when we change churches. Our excitement and eagerness for work quickly vanishes when the reality of work and the associated difficulties with it begin to surface. For some this can happen quickly, for others it can take place over a long period of time. Whenever our expectations surpass job reality but don't reach a balance after a certain period of time, we begin to undergo the anxiety of unattainable expectations. The following are examples of how job realities can differ from job expectations.

Expectation: Work will be stimulating, adventuresome, and rewarding experience.
Reality: Work is normally very boring and predictable.
Expectation: As pastor, I will be part of the decision making process, using my skills, abilities, and intellect.
Reality: The deacons and committees make the decisions.
Expectation: As pastor, I will be able to lead the con-

gregation to be God's best.

Reality: Many will not follow the lead of the pastor.

These are only a few ways expectation and job realities do not match the real world. Many times the standards we set for ourselves are too high. If we realize that we are not going to reach those standards we need to lower our standards. If we do not, we are headed for burnout. *Check out the burnout barometer in the appendix to determine if you are in a burnout phase.*

When reality finally sets in, how do we cope with the fact that our expectations many never turn into realities? Instead of becoming depressed, we can begin to adjust to reality by accepting certain facts about work. Reality is always going to be a disappointment at first unless we accept the task and do something positive concerning the expectation. In most cases, work is something we fit into not the job fitting us. We can choose to make work a pleasant or unpleasant experience through the power of our mind. We must set realistic goals that are attainable and at the same time receive satisfaction from our work. The alternative is to become progressively less productive and of less benefit to loved ones and to yourself as a result of burnout.

Pastor's Interpersonal Skills

After interviewing three men who serve as consultants in the area of church-minister relations, one common denominator surfaced as a factor in forced terminations; the minister's interpersonal skills. The most frequent complaint about clergy who were forced to terminate was that "they could not get along with people."

Those dismissed were perceived by some as authoritarian, withdrawn, uncaring, difficult, or passive in their relationships with church members.

In his monograph, Speed Leas from the Alban Institute shares the following criteria as signs of a lack of interpersonal competence:

1. The pastor does not understand the situation, especially what he/she does to make it worse.

2. The pastor places the blame entirely on other persons or groups.

3. The pastor is unable to delegate appropriately, either abdicating responsibility or not allowing others to take responsibility.

4. The pastor is unable to develop common commitments and loyalties within the congregation, tending to be divisive, using separating tactics, rather than using integrative, pull-together tactics.

5. The pastor is unable to make clear, direct statements and behave in a way consistent with those statements. (The pastor says he/she will do one thing and then does something else, or the pastor implies he/she is for something and then shows by his/her behavior that he/she is not.)

6. The pastor does not support others emotionally when disagreeing with them intellectually.

7. The pastor needs emotional support and approval all the time from everybody to feel comfortable about himself/herself.

8. The pastor is not able to interpret what is happening in the present based on reality. (A pastor unable to handle this situation is likely to see all the questions as survival questions or will impose on the present that which is expected from the future rather than what is actually happening.)

9. The pastor treats differentness as a threat or signal to conflict rather than an opportunity to learn.

10. The pastor does not accept the responsibility for what he/she feels, thinks, hears, or sees but rather denies responsibility for what is happening and attributes it to others.[3]

Many pastors have a difficult time relating to others because of the pedestal barrier, where the pastor is seen as one who cannot ever have problems. This causes many pastors to become self-enclosed and silent about their own personal battles in life. Asking for help from the laity would seem unfitting, especially since the pastor is to be seen as the spiritual leader. Therefore, some pastors allow themselves to be consumed by their work, becoming constrained by the fear of criticism. The result is that the pastor will not allow himself to establish relationships based on the mutual accessibility and candor needed to maintain open communication. By closing himself off, the minister can lose credibility with the laity.

The Pastor's Personality not Matching the Church's Personality

At times, conflict can arise when the identity of the pastor does not fit the church. Sometimes the difference is cultural (The pastor may be from the south and the congregation is distinctly northern). Or, the pastor may identify with a particular social class while the congregation identifies with another. Appreciation of different music styles seems to be a cause for conflict between many churches and their pastors. When mismatches occur, the prevailing attitude is that the pastor is not one of "us," but one of "them."

My last pastorate was one that expected the pastor to look and act, as a "typical" pastor should, with the black suit and short hair cut. My personality is one that differs from most "typical" pastors. In fact, my disposition is one that is very contrary to the "model" pastor. I have a very active lifestyle, which includes flying airplanes, skydiving, playing a guitar in a praise band, and riding Harley Davidson motorcycles. These activities were accepted by most, but the "old guard" leadership of the church did not approve of my "unrestrained" lifestyle.

Prior to my resignation, some deacons told me that they never did like me because I had an airplane and rode a Harley. The reality hit me that most pastors are really seen as a third gender; male, female, and preachers. We as preachers are not to have a life outside of preaching, visiting, praying, and administering the ordinances of the church.

For eight years, I tried to get the leadership to accept me as God had wired me up, but my personality did not match the expectation of the leadership of the church. Even when I tried to please them by changing my personality, I was not accepted. I learned that I had failed to change the status quo concerning the acceptance of a pastor.

So, pastor, before you go to the next church, check out the personality of that church. Call previous pastors and ask them what the church is like, or even pastors in the same ministry area. If your temperament is not even close to the expectations of the majority, you will have a difficult struggle trying to minister in a mismatched environment.

Unhealthy Lay Leadership

Every church has members who are considered "key" people in the congregation. If these members truly serve Christ and follow the Biblical example of conflict management, the pastor will not have too much trouble with the leadership in the church. If, on the other hand, the key leadership is unhealthy, then the pastor will have a very difficult time when it comes to any disagreement.

Even if a few key leaders are unhealthy, the pastor and church will experience grief. One pastor in Kentucky explained to me that he had two deacons that "ran" the church for years. The first time he had a conflict with them, they warned him that "they will string him up in the tree in the parking lot if he did not listen to them." The young pastor left the church within a few months.

A pastor must watch for distorted thinking from lay leadership and, when identified, confront it immediately. If allowed to fester, it will move throughout the congregation.

In their book *Emotional Well-Being Through Rational Behavior Training,* David Goodman and Maxie Maultsby list categories of distorted thinking:

1. Inconsistency: The person expects high standards from himself or others some times, and not at others.

2. The NonSequitur: His reasoning has gaps in it — hence the use of the term *non sequitur,* Latin for "it doesn't follow." He concludes that he will not believe what someone says because they have long hair or are late for an appointment.

3. Generalizing from a Few Particulars: The person makes general conclusions based on a few isolated facts, as in the case of deciding that all persons belonging to a certain group have qualities that he has found in one or two members of that group.

4. Exaggeration: The person describes a moderate failure as a catastrophe or an inconvenience as a terrible problem.

5. Building a Case: The person selects only those observations about someone or something that fits his preconceived conclusions - favorable or unfavorable.

6. Shifting Responsibility: Instead of assessing responsibility for a given situation to one or more possible causes, the person arbitrarily assigns it to a person he has selected or a condition he has decided, in advance, is the cause.

7. Viewing Feelings as Facts: The person believes that because he reacts to something or someone in a certain way that is emotional, this means, therefore, that something or someone actually is the way he views them.

8. Viewing Memories as Present-Day Realities: The person persists in thinking, feeling, and acting today as if certain past events or conditions were still in effect and still governing his behavior.

9. Perceiving Remote Possibilities as Imminent Probabilities: The person fails to distinguish between these two very different situations. He cannot see the difference between "could" and "is likely to."

10. Trying to Reconstruct Reality: The person thinks in the "as if" mode, declaring that a person or situation "should" be different than it is, simply because he wants it to be that way, failing to recognize the antecedents for something being the way it is.

11. Expecting Immediate or Rapid Change: Impatience, in itself, can lead to irrational conclusions about the speed of changes in situations or other's or one's own behavior. The emotional desire for change interferes with clear perception as to its feasibility and its speed.

12. Following Established Habit Patterns: The satisfaction derived from repeating behavior interferes with

clear perception as to whether the behavior is personally or socially desirable. The person reasons that because a behavior was gratifying in the past, therefore, it deserves to be repeated in the future, regardless of consequences.

13. Assuming One's Behavior is Externally Caused: This assumes a direct relationship between outside events and one's own feelings, thoughts or actions, ignoring one's own role in creating behavior.

14. Assuming One is Responsible for Whatever Happens: This is the opposite of No. 13 above and is based on the arbitrary concept of self-blame, rather than an objective weighing of various causes. This is also the opposite of No. 6, wherein one shifts responsibility to others arbitrarily, resulting in "other-blame," and ultimately paranoia.

15. Perfectionism: The person thinks in terms of "always," "never," "have to" and "must not" with respect to his own behavior and that of others, or in regard to conditions and situations he either insisted be achieved or demands be maintained. He does not recognize fallibility as an inescapable quality of human beings.

16. Magical Thinking: The person believes that something will or might happen because he dreams, feels, or thinks that it should, according to some preconceived "system" of ideas he has adopted. Astrology, superstition, witchcraft, and other arbitrary ideolo-

gies are classic examples of the magical way of perceiving and interpreting the world.

17. Mindreading: The person believes he can "feel" what other people are thinking or that they can feel what he is thinking. He thus imagines reactions that may be totally at variance with reality.[4]

Difficult Church History

Larry McSwain, in his book *Conflict Ministry in the Church* explains that churches having a history of disruptive conflict are churches, which will have the greatest difficulty becoming healthy, with congregations capable of handling conflict constructively.[5] Factions may go back many years to a church split, an old decision about building a new building, a theological difference, or family feuds. In my study of forced terminations, I have found that many pastors who are in churches with a difficult church history are more likely to have to resign than pastors in churches with a history of being willing to work out the disagreements.

From their research, the Alban Institute shares that with 43% of the pastors forced to terminate, dynamics were present within the congregation itself, which inhibited or destroyed the possibility of effective pastoral leadership.[6] In my last pastorate I discovered that since 1906 I was the third longest tenured pastor. The average stay of a pastor over the past 91 years had been two years or less.

One lady who had been in the church for over 70 years shared a story concerning her first pastor in the church. He was a schoolteacher that gave his time to the church, receiving no salary at all. When he needed some extra money, he decided to tutor a few students in the community. When the deacons found out about the tutoring they approached the pastor, explaining that he would have to resign because he did not spend enough time "on the field."

Following my forced resignation, the sad church member explained that this has been the history of the church as long as she can remember. The history of the church has proven that they are unwilling to identify problems early and to work through them with the pastor. It is much easier to force the pastor to leave and ignore the problem.

If the pastor had conflict with just one individual, he would be able to confront that person one on one. The problem most pastors face is that every congregation is made up of not only individuals but also groups.

In their book *Church Conflicts, The Hidden System Behind the Fights*, Charles Cosgrove and Dennis Hatfield share the concept that churches are like families. They believe that people replicate family patterns that they learned while growing up.[7] Each church, like a family has a personality and a way of dealing with conflict. Some churches are known to be supportive and nurturing to their pastor and his family. Normally, when a pastor feels cared for and a part of the church family, the tenure is lengthy.

When a church family is dysfunctional, they prefer to keep their pastor in the box of the ministerial office, allowing him only a marginal place in the family. Outside the identity of the pastoral office, the minister feels excluded.

In a healthy church the pastor is seen as the "undershepherd," even as the parent in the family. In years past, the office of the pastor carried the parental authority in the church family. When conflict occurred, it was the pastor who settled the dispute; he was the parent in the church family.

In the dysfunctional church, the pastor does not carry the role as parent. The pastor who does not become a parent in the family is in a very weak position when dealing with congregational conflict and participating effectively in church decision- making.[8]

When the minister is not part of the church family, it reminds me of a police officer trying to handle a domestic disturbance. I have served as a volunteer chaplain for our county Sheriff's Patrol for the past seven years. I have learned that trying to break up a family squabble can be very dangerous. In fact, once the officer is called in, squabbles between husbands and wives change very quickly. The wrath of both husband and wife are turned toward the innocent party, the officer, because he has become an infringement on their privacy.

In a similar way, when the pastor is not a part of the family, he is seen as an infringement upon the church family having a squabble. The parties that have had conflict with one another can even unite, combining forces to vent their wrath on the new invader, the pastor.

I would suggest to the new pastor that he work toward becoming part of the family; the more dysfunctional the church is, the more time it will take, if it is possible at all. The best way is to join through affirmation and identification. The pastor cannot treat the church family like a foster child; he must get involved and make them feel that he truly cares for them. As you affirm members, you bring value to them. In identifying with a group, we look for ways in which we are similar. Adopting the ways of the family, especially at the beginning, is another way of identification.

In my second church, there was a family tradition of having a drive-by nativity scene complete with costumes, animals, and music. I honestly did not like the idea of standing in sub-zero weather with a camel breathing down my neck as people drove by looking at me in a costume. I did realize that this was something the church looked forward to every year. I made the decision to allow myself to be a part of the family tradition. So, there I was with hot chocolate in hand, my toes freezing, a camel behind me and a donkey standing by my side. The church loved the fact that I would become a part of their tradition and it helped me to be accepted as a genuine family member.

Staff Infection

The one area that always has the potential for conflict is with the church staff. Any group of people working together are certain to experience some degree of tension and conflict from time to time. Personality clashes, personal goals, and ambitions can all create controversy. A staff that works well together takes time, energy, and most of all, care for each other.

The senior pastor must always be the servant leader of the staff. He must lead by example and guide the staff to minister to the congregation. Weekly staff meeting are vital as the pastor makes sure the members of the staff are moving together as a team in following the cast vision.

Loyalty is the golden word in staff relations. If the staff is not loyal to the pastor, he will surely fail. I have had to deal with staff members who tried to create their own church within the church, who manufactured and shared rumors, and who wanted to take over as pastor. If this type of behavior is not dealt with immediately, the pastor will have even greater conflict. When the pastor pulls away or withdraws from the problem, he is seen as one that doesn't really care.

Physical withdrawal is seen when the pastor simply stays away from the staff, or accepts frequent invitations to speak at other locations. Mental withdrawal involves watching too much TV, daydreaming, sleeping too much or escaping with alcohol or drugs. These types of reaction will create a larger burden later.

When staff members disagree with a pastor they should go to him directly instead of running to a deacon or board member or holding secret meetings. Often personnel committees conspire with staff to make matters worse. Every time a board or personnel committee meets with one staff person alone for the purpose of discussing the pastor or another staff person it makes it more difficult to deal with problems in the relationship.[10]

One of the greatest errors I made was to follow the advice of a personnel committee chairman and not have contact with any of the staff. This enhances the separation of the staff and pastor; it does not help them confront one another and work through their differences.

Unclear Lines of Authority

Brooks Faulkner in his book, *Forced Termination,*

Redemptive Options for Ministers and Churches says that there should be no competition for the position of pastor. It will be confusing to leadership and followers if there is not a leader.[11] If an associate aspires to become a senior pastor, he should clearly explain that to the pastor and clear lines of responsibility should be drawn. If the pastor senses competition for the position of pastor, he should immediately confront the associate about his ambition.

A church staff and a marriage are very similar. One of the most difficult aspects in marriage is deciding who is the leader and who has the power in the family. If the husband and wife follow the Biblical teachings, there is mutual respect between the husband and wife, yet someone must be the leader. The same is true with the staff and the church family. There must be mutual respect, openness, honesty, and togetherness, but there must be a leader.

Good marriages don't just happen; neither do good relationships with the staff and church. The relationship is a result of what each person brings to the setting. There must be a clear understanding of who is in charge as the pastor rules, not with an iron fist, but leads in love.

END NOTES

[1] Speed B. Leas, *Moving Your Church Through Conflict* (Washington, D.C.: The Alban Institute, Inc., 1985), 80.

[2] John C. Harris, *Stress, Power and Ministry* (Washington, D.C.: The Alban Institute Inc., 1977), 57.

[3] Speed B. Leas, *Should the Pastor Be Fired?* (Washington, D.C.: The Alban Institute Inc., 1980), 9-10.

[4] David S. Goodman and Maxie C. Maultsby, Jr., *Emotional Well-Being Through Rational Behavior Training* (Springfield: Charles C Thomas Publisher, 1978) , 41-42.

[5] Larry L. McSwain, *Conflict Ministry in the Church.* (Nashville: Broadman Press, 1981), 70.

[6] Leas, *Should the Pastor Be Fired?*, 10.

[7] Charles H. Cosgrove and Dennis D. Hatfield, *Church Conflict, The Hidden System Behind the Fights.* (Nashville: Abingdon Press, 1994), 12.

[8] Ibid., 184.

[9] Brooks Faulkner, *Stress in the Life of the Minister.* (Nashville: Convention Press, 1981) 98.

[10] Leas, *Moving Your Church Through Conflict,* 80.

[11] Brooks Faulkner, *Forced Termination, Redemptive Options for Ministers and Churches.* (Nashville: Broadman Press, 1986). 56.

CHAPTER FOUR

What Does the Bible Say?

Throughout his earthly ministry, Jesus Christ had to constantly deal with opposition and conflict. Resistance by the religious leaders of his day was a constant battle. They opposed who he claimed to be, his message, and his leadership. There are numerous conflict examples in the Sermon on the Mount (Matthew 5-7). Several times in his message Jesus declares, "You have heard that it was said," and, "But I tell you." Jesus was misquoted, misinterpreted, and lied about, which led to conflict.

Conflict is not new to the church. Scripture records many conflicts and honestly reports their outcomes, whether favorable or unfavorable.[1] In this chapter I will give accounts that relate to conflict episodes and what we can learn from them. I will also share at the end of the chapter the importance of restoration as seen in the scripture.

Conflict and the Gospels
Matthew 20:1-16

"For the kingdom of heaven is like a landowner who went out early in the morning to hire men to work in his vineyard. He agreed to pay them a denarius for the day and sent them into his vineyard.

"About the third hour he went out and saw others standing in the marketplace doing nothing. He told them, 'You also go and work in my vineyard, and I will pay you whatever is right.' So they went.

"He went out again about the sixth hour and the ninth hour and did the same thing. About the eleventh hour he went out and found still others standing around. He asked them, 'Why have you been standing here all day long doing nothing?'

" 'Because no one has hired us,' they answered.

"He said to them, 'You also go and work in my vineyard.'

"When evening came, the owner of the vineyard said to his foreman, 'Call the workers and pay them their wages, beginning with the last ones hired and going on to the first.'

"The workers who were hired about the eleventh hour came and each received a denarius. So when those came who were hired first, they expected to receive more. But each one of them also received a denarius. When they received it, they began to grumble against the landowner. 'These men who were hired last worked only one hour,' they said, 'and you have made them equal to us who have borne the burden of the work and the heat of the day.'

"But he answered one of them, 'Friend, I am not being unfair to you. Didn't you agree to work for a denarius? Take your pay and go. I want to give the man who was hired last the same as I gave you. Don't I have the right to do what I want with my own money? Or are you envious because I am generous?'

"So the last will be first, and the first will be last."

The issue focused on felt justice. The owner had one expectation of payment, the workers had an entirely different view. What we can learn from this recorded conflict is that we view the conflict from our limited frame of reference. Sadly, we normally make little effort to understand how someone else may view the information.

The character of some of the workers also led to conflict, as the Biblical story shows. Those complaining had a legitimate contract. If the owner decided to be generous to those he hired later, that was totally his choice. Dissatisfaction existed because some workers made the payroll their business rather than accepting their contract as agreed upon.

Luke 10:38-42

As Jesus and his disciples were on their way, he came to a village where a woman named Martha opened her home to him. She had a sister called Mary, who sat at the Lord's feet listening to what he said. But Martha was distracted by all the preparations that had to be made. She came to him and asked, "Lord, don't you care that my sister has left me to do the work by myself? Tell her to help me!"

"Martha, Martha," the Lord answered, "you are worried and upset about many things, but only one thing is needed. Mary has chosen what is better, and it will not be taken away from her."

Mary and Martha both had good objectives in mind. Martha was a hard worker, a commendable trait, while

Mary wanted to be near Jesus — that we applaud. The conflict arose when Martha determined that Mary had made an unfavorable choice.

What we can learn from the Biblical narrative is that sometimes we transfer our goals and objectives to other believers. Mary and Martha were both doing good things. Like Martha, we become more excitable when we *know* what we are doing is right. We all know good Christian people who like to set guidelines for everyone else to live by. If the person they are forcing the guidelines upon does not properly follow through, he is looked upon with disdain.

At times we can identify with Martha, especially if we feel unappreciated. At times, conflict will arise because one person feels others in the church are getting more attention; like a child, this person's actions say "look at me, not them."

We must learn to focus our attention on Jesus, rather than forcing our goals and objectives on others. Jesus wants us to listen and understand him, instead of focusing on tasks.

Luke 22:24-27

Also a dispute arose among them as to which of them was considered to be greatest. Jesus said to them, "The kings of the Gentiles lord it over them; and those who exercise authority over them call themselves Benefactors. But you are not to be like that. Instead, the greatest among you should be like the youngest, and the one who rules like the one who serves. For who is greater, the one who is at the table or the one who serves? Is it not the one who is at the table? But I am among you as one who serves."

This conflict discloses the problem of role definition and position. Each of the disciples wanted to be viewed as more important than the others. How often do we see conflict arise out of positioning in the church? One person desires to be chairman of the personnel committee, or some related committee, so he can feel important and powerful over others.

Conflict can help unveil ambitions that drive us to climb the ladder of success. Wanting to feel important and jockeying for position are common causes of conflict in the local church. By what standard do we assess greatness? As we read the scripture it is clear that being a servant-leader is what is great in the eyes of God. The more we strive to be like Jesus, the less we will be concerned with greatness.

John 12:1-8

Six days before the Passover, Jesus arrived at Bethany, where Lazarus lived, whom Jesus had raised from the dead. Here a dinner was given in Jesus' honor. Martha served, while Lazarus was among those reclining at the table with him. Then Mary took about a pint of pure nard, an expensive perfume; she poured it on Jesus' feet and wiped his feet with her hair. And the house was filled with the fragrance of the perfume.

But one of his disciples, Judas Iscariot, who was later to betray him, objected, "Why wasn't this perfume sold and the money given to the poor? It was worth a year's wages." He did not say this because he cared about the poor but because he was a thief; as keeper of the money bag, he used to help himself to what was put into it.

"Leave her alone," Jesus replied. "It was intended that she should save this perfume for the day of my burial. You will always have the poor among you, but you will not always have me."

The conflict issue in this scripture deals with values. Judas put a high value on the possible money this perfume would bring. Jesus defended the lady with the perfume because she had a better set of values. Conflict sometimes has a right side and a wrong side; we do not always experience a win-win situation.[2] When we listen to God and follow His Word, we must follow the scripture if we are going to be on the right side.

Judas reveals a hidden agenda in this recorded conflict. He was contemplating what he could steal, and the perfume could have brought him more money if sold. Hidden agendas quickly appear when conflict leads to the communication process. In my situation, I had two on the staff that wanted to be the pastor, so it was easy for them to not defend me when it was time to find reasons for me to leave. In fact, I later found out that the same two staff members led the dissension from the beginning. Our values always surface when conflict arises.

John 21:15-19

When they had finished eating, Jesus said to Simon Peter, "Simon son of John, do you truly love me more than these?"

"Yes, Lord," he said, "you know that I love you."

Jesus said, "Feed my lambs."

Again Jesus said, "Simon son of John, do you truly love me?"

He answered, "Yes, Lord, you know that I love you."

Jesus said, "Take care of my sheep."

The third time he said to him, "Simon son of John, do you love me?"

Peter was hurt because Jesus asked him the third time, "Do you love me?" He said, "Lord, you know all things; you know that I love you."

Jesus said, "Feed my sheep. I tell you the truth, when you were younger you dressed yourself and went where you wanted; but when you are old you will stretch out your hands, and someone else will dress you and lead you where you do not want to go." Jesus said this to indicate the kind of death by which Peter would glorify God. Then he said to him, "Follow me!"

Jesus shows Peter that conflict focuses on past performance. Peter had previously denied the Lord, and now Jesus was asking him repeatedly if he meant what he said. After Peter denied Jesus, the scriptural accounts show, he did not live a life of arrogance again. He learned that he was responsible for his words and actions.

Conflict can truly be a learning experience if we are not blinded by our desired outcome (to win). As I look back over recent conflict, I realize that if I evaluate the process, I can learn about my normal pattern of dealing with difficulty. With God's help, the pattern can be changed to parallel the scripture as conflict arises.

Conflict and the Epistles

Romans 12:9-21

Love must be sincere. Hate what is evil; cling to what is good. Be devoted to one another in brotherly love. Honor one another above yourselves. Never be lacking in zeal, but keep your spiritual fervor, serving the Lord. Be joyful in hope, patient in affliction, faithful in prayer. Share with God's people who are in need. Practice hospitality.

Bless those who persecute you; bless and do not curse. Rejoice with those who rejoice; mourn with those who mourn. Live in harmony with one another. Do not be proud, but be willing to associate with people of low position. Do not be conceited.

Do not repay anyone evil for evil. Be careful to do what is right in the eyes of everybody. If it is possible, as far as it depends on you, live at peace with everyone. Do not take revenge, my friends, but leave room for God's wrath, for it is written: "It is mine to avenge; I will repay," says the Lord. On the contrary:

"If your enemy is hungry, feed him; if he is thirsty, give him something to drink.

In doing this, you will heap burning coals on his head."

Do not be overcome by evil, but overcome evil with good.

This passage focuses on the command for believers to be at peace with all men. There is a mandate for believers to work toward harmony. The passage also speaks of Christians treating each other with respect, not pursuing revenge. The world's way of handling conflict is to get revenge — to "get back" at the person creating the controversy. When we are engaged in conflict, we must determine if we are identifying with the actions conducive to a Christian or the actions of the world.

1 Corinthians 6:1-8

If any of you has a dispute with another, dare he take it before the ungodly for judgment instead of before the saints? Do you not know that the saints will judge the world? And if you are to judge the world, are you not competent to judge trivial cases? Do you not know that we will judge angels? How much more the things of this life! Therefore, if you have disputes about such matters, appoint as judges even men of little account in the church! I say this to shame you. Is it possible that there is nobody among you wise enough to judge a dispute between believers? But instead, one brother goes to law against another — and this in front of unbelievers!

The very fact that you have lawsuits among you means you have been completely defeated already. Why not rather be wronged? Why not rather be cheated? Instead, you yourselves cheat and do wrong, and you do this to your brothers.

This passage shows that there is a legitimate judicial function in any body of believers. The question to be answered is, how quickly should the church go to outside arbitration? This passage shares that the church should adjudicate their own problems.

Galatians 2:11-21

When Peter came to Antioch, I opposed him to his face, because he was clearly in the wrong. Before certain men came from James, he used to eat with the Gentiles. But when they arrived, he began to draw back and separate himself from the Gentiles because he was afraid of those who belonged to the circumcision group. The other Jews joined him in his hypocrisy, so that by their hypocrisy even Barnabas was led astray.

When I saw that they were not acting in line with the truth of the gospel, I said to Peter in front of them all, "You are a Jew, yet you live like a Gentile and not like a Jew. How is it, then, that you force Gentiles to follow Jewish customs?"

"We who are Jews by birth and not 'Gentile sinners' know that a man is not justified by observing the law, but by faith in Jesus Christ. So we, too, have put our faith in Christ Jesus that we may be justified by faith in Christ and not by observing the law, because by observing the law no one will be justified."

"If, while we seek to be justified in Christ, it becomes evident that we ourselves are sinners, does that mean that Christ promotes sin? Absolutely not! If I rebuild what I destroyed, I prove that I am a lawbreaker. For through the law I died to the law so that I might live for God. I have been crucified with Christ and I no longer live, but Christ lives in me. The life I live in the body, I live by faith in the Son of God, who loved me and gave himself for me. I do not set aside the grace of God, for if righteousness could be gained through the law, Christ died for nothing!"

Paul demonstrates the importance of all parties present when the conflict is discussed. No parties should be denied the opportunity to be a part of the conflict process. When a pastor is not allowed into the meetings where he is being discussed, it is a clear violation of scripture, especially when the pastor does not have the opportunity to defend himself.

I have spoken with several pastors who have been forced to terminate, and the majority explain that there were secret meetings held and decisions made without their knowledge. By the time they had the opportunity to make a defense, irreparable damage had been done.

Conflict and Church Leadership

Unfortunately, not every instance of conflict in the New Testament has a pleasurable result. At times, those in spiritual leadership had sharp contrasts when it came to doing ministry. For example, Paul and Barnabas conflicted when they were trying to make a decision about whether or not to include young John Mark on one of their missionary journeys. John had left them on a previous missionary trip, and Paul saw him as incompetent for missionary service. Barnabus, Mark's uncle, saw it differently.

Neither Paul or Barnabus would change their position, resulting in a successful missionary team going their separate ways. Paul chose Silas as his partner, and Barnabus took John Mark. This account is found in Acts 15:36-41.

On another occasion in Antioch, Paul was upset with Barnabus, accusing both him and Peter of giving ear to those who thought circumcision a prerequisite to salvation. Paul's intention was to be direct, which at times resulted in severed relationships. Throughout Paul's writings, we see him wrestling with the ageless and potentially explosive problem of when to engage in principle-centered conflict and when to be charitable.[3] Paul counsels his readers to avoid conflict over minor matters; however, he is vehement in defending principles that he considers sacred. In First Corinthians 5:9-13, Paul provides stern instructions concerning the lifestyle of a Christian.

I have written you in my letter not to associate with sexually immoral people — not at all meaning the people of this world who are immoral, or the greedy and swindlers, or idolaters. In that case you would have to leave this world. But now I am writing you that you must not associate with anyone who calls himself a brother but is sexually immoral or greedy, an idolater or a slanderer, a drunkard or a swindler. With such a man do not even eat.

What business is it of mine to judge those outside the church? Are you not to judge those inside? God will judge those outside. "Expel the wicked man from among you."

Later in Paul's ministry, he penned some beautiful words in the promotion of peace. There is a very caring heart seen in the writings:

To the Corinthians: "I appeal to you, brothers, in the name of our Lord Jesus Christ, that all of you agree with one another so that there may be no divisions among you and that you may be perfectly united in mind and thought." (1 Cor. 1:10)

To the Ephesians: "Get rid of all bitterness, rage and anger, brawling and slander, along with every form of malice. Be kind and compassionate to one another, forgiving each other, just as in Christ God forgave you." (Eph. 4:31-32)

To the Philippians: "If you have any encouragement from being united with Christ, if any comfort from his love, if any fellowship with the Spirit, if any tenderness and compassion, then make my joy complete by being like-minded, having the same love, being one in spirit and purpose. Do nothing out of selfish ambition or vain conceit, but in humility consider others better than yourselves. Each of you should look not only to your own interests, but also to the interests of others." (Phil. 2:1-4)

To the Colossians: "Therefore, as God's chosen people, holy and dearly loved, clothe yourselves with compassion, kindness, humility, gentleness and patience. Bear with each other and forgive whatever grievances you may have against one another. Forgive as the Lord forgave you. And over all these virtues put on love, which binds them all together in perfect unity." (Col. 3:12-14)

To the Thessalonians: "Now about brotherly love we do not need to write to you, for you yourselves have been taught by God to love each other. And in fact, you do love all the brothers throughout Macedonia. Yet we urge you, brothers, to do so more and more. Make it your ambition to lead a quiet life, to mind your own business and to work with your hands, just as we told you, so that your daily life may win the respect of outsiders and so that you will not be dependent on anybody." (1 Thess. 4:9-11)

Allowing the Scripture to guide us may not enable us to always prevent conflict. However, if we follow the Scripture it will guide us in how conflict is to be conducted, and possibly in how it can be resolved properly.

Biblical Resolution

The Bible is clear on how conflict is to be handled among believers. In Matthew 18:15-17, Jesus shares guidelines on how to deal with conflict with a brother in Christ. If church members would follow the principles of priority as seen in Matthew 18, less conflict would take place, and the body of Christ would be able to make a difference in their respective communities.

In most cases, we as Christians handle conflict the way the person outside the church does. Depending on our personality, we may use coercive tactics where we *bully* the person we are having conflict with. Physical, psychological, social, or even spiritual "rank-pulling" are examples of how this coercive tactic functions. Or, trying to escape conflict, we may even ignore or compromise just to find some type of peace.

As Christians, we are mandated by our Lord to handle conflict in a spiritual manner. In obedience to God's holy word, we must follow the principles of priority as seen in Matthew 18:15-17.

First Step

I will do as Matthew 18 admonishes — go to an offending brother "first alone." I must not share the offense with another person. I must be committed to restoring the relationship rather than exposing possible sin. Most problems are personality clashes. As we try to understand the actions of others, trying to see the friction from their perspective, we can avoid conflict.

Second Step

If going to a person "first alone" does not resolve the conflict, I must promise to seek a neutral and mature individual who will listen to each side, and hopefully shed light on the problem, leading to resolution. I must recognize that this person might reveal things I may not like, but I must believe that God is using this person to help resolve the conflict rather than take sides.

I must not seek to find another person who has also been offended. The purpose of having a "witness" is not to validate my hurt, but rather to open my heart and mind to possible deficiencies I may have regarding my relationship with others.

I realize that my friends may naturally listen and take my side. Therefore, I will not cause them to become a party to a possible division and disharmony because of our friendship. I must commune with God concerning my hurt, allowing Him to heal my hurts.

Final Step

If taking a witness does not resolve the problem, we are admonished to "tell it to the church." This section of Scripture may be talking about the entire church body, or the leadership of the church. The point being made is that nothing is ever settled by Christless arguments. It is in an atmosphere of Christian prayer, Christian love and Christian fellowship that personal relationships may be made right. The clear assumption is that the church fellowship is Christian, and seeks to judge everything, not in the light of a book of practices and procedures, but in the light of love. Of course, this only works if the leadership chooses to see the conflict through the eyes of love and compassion.

The Scripture continues, "... and if he refuses to listen even to the church, treat him as you would a pagan or a tax collector." The first impression is that the man must be abandoned as hopeless and irreclaimable. In other Scriptures, Jesus never set limits on human forgiveness. What then did he mean?

When Jesus speaks of tax-gatherers and sinners, he always does it with sympathy and gentleness and an appreciation of their good qualities. It may be that Jesus meant when the person has been given every chance and he remains stubborn, he may be seen as no better than a renegade tax collector, or even a godless pagan. However, Jesus never found tax collectors and pagans hopeless. He believed they too had hearts that needed to be touched; many of them, like Matthew and Zacchaeus, became good friends, to Jesus. Even if the person being brought before the leadership is stubborn, we are not to abandon him; instead, we are challenged to win him with the love, which can touch even the hardest heart. Jesus Christ has found no man hopeless — and neither must we.

Confronting Ministry Leaders

We are admonished by the Scripture not to rebuke an Elder (spiritual leader), other than grave matters of misconduct and *open* sin (1 Timothy 5:19). Each church member should earnestly pray for and follow the spiritual leaders that God has placed over them. Church members should not allow anyone to criticize their spiritual leaders without following the principles in Matthew 18.

If a church member has a problem with their ministry leader, they must go "first alone" to them. They are not to share their concern with others. If the church member is not satisfied with the meeting, they should ask their spiritual leader for permission and counsel to find a "witness" who will listen to the conflict.

If the witness finds that the church member has misunderstood the situation, they should continue no further, and trust God by casting the burden on the Lord and leaving it there. If the witness agrees with the concern of the church member, and the ministry leader refuses to hear the witness, there needs to be a group of two or three other witnesses who will hear the matter and determine what God is doing through the conflict. These "witnesses" must be neutral and mature individuals that the ministry leader and church member agree upon.

If the church member continues to find fault with the ministry leader and cannot worship in "spirit and truth," they should seek to join another ministry rather than causing disharmony within the church body. Separating from the source of irritation can allow the church member to worship God in another ministry setting.

Christians must commit themselves to being spiritual rather than normal when it comes to solving problems with others. The ultimate goal of every Christian is to glorify God through bearing much fruit, getting involved in ministry, and avoiding and resolving conflict.

Restoring Broken Brothers

In Galatians 6:1 the Apostle Paul writes: *Brothers, if someone is caught in a sin, you who are spiritual should restore him gently. But watch yourself, or you also may be tempted.* The Bible is clear that we are to restore one fallen in sin gently and in a spiritual manner. The apostle uses the word *katartizo* to describe the goal of restoration. The Greek word katartizo means to mend or repair. The idea is the setting of a broken bone, or putting a dislocated limb back in place.

Galatians 6 carries the idea that we are not to hurt the offender, but help him. Treat him as you yourselves would wish to be treated if you were in his place. I suggest to deacons and church leaders that you need to seek the complete recovery of the fallen individual. The fallen Christian's forgiveness before God must be acknowledged. As he repents, it must be accepted. Sadly, many church leaders do not follow the admonition from Scripture to restore a fallen brother. The church has historically dealt more kindly with converted sinners who previously lived in reckless moral abandon than with members who later backslide into sinful living. When we accept Christ, we are called to separate ourselves from the world and live holy lives. When a follower of Christ turns back to the world, there are consequences.

As we restore fallen members, we must be gentle because we ourselves can fall the same way. If we as leaders are arrogant, faultfinding and give the impression of spiritual superiority, we will hurt the process of restoring the fallen brother. When the fallen brother comes before the leadership with genuine repentance, we must move toward restoration in love. The ultimate goal is always to glorify God.

END NOTES

[1] Huttenlocker, Keith, *Conflict and Caring*, (Grand Rapids: Zondervan Publishing House, 1988), 132.

[2] Gangel, Kenneth O., and Canine, Samuel L., *Communication and Conflict Management*, Nashville: Broadman Press, 1992). 170.

[3] Huttenlocker, *Conflict and Caring*, 135.

[4] Armstrong, John H., *Can Fallen Pastors be Restored?* (Chicago: Moody Press, 1995). 162.

CHAPTER FIVE

Identifying the Stages of Conflict That Lead to Forced Termination

When a pastor is forced to resign, there are normally stages of conflict seen prior to the severing of leadership. The conflict between pastor and people unfolds in at least five stages; early warning signs, dissension and polarization, contests of wills, solidifying factions, and destroying the other.

Stage 1 — Early Warning Signs

Complaints

Perhaps the most frequent early warning sign of conflict is the presence of members complaining to one another about the pastor. These complaints can be about anything; the pastor's hobbies, his sermons, the way he dresses, the type of car he drives, the kind of house he lives in, his leadership style, his participation in the denomination, etc. These and many other complaints can be expressed directly or indirectly. Many times, the complaints are vague. As the pastor hears the complaints, he has the opportunity to identify and deal with the sources of irritation within the church body.

Ideally, members should come to the pastor directly

as discussed in chapter four. In my experience, most people who complain will not complain directly to the person they are upset with, especially the pastor. The pastor should take a respected leader within the church and, in a gentle spirit, confront the person complaining, trying to resolve the differences. If the pastor ignores the complaints, they will continue to grow within the church body.

Rumors

One of the most damaging early warning signs are rumors, especially if they concern the character of the pastor. Many pastors have left their position because a rumor was not dealt with early, allowing the untruth to have a snowball effect throughout the congregation. What is amazing is that so many people believe the rumors without even checking the validity of such hearsay.

Pastor, you must deal with the rumor immediately. Find the source of the rumor and confront the person at once. Hopefully, the person will apologize and work through the relationship by the Scriptural guidelines. I suggest that you ask the person who they have talked to and make sure that the truth is communicated the right away.

Withdrawal

Another early warning sign is the withdrawal of certain members from one another or from the pastor. At the beginning, this withdrawal can be as subtle as a couple leaving the church by another door rather than shaking the pastor's hand.

The pastor may also avoid certain members because they seem cold or make him feel uncomfortable. Often, the pastor is labeled as one that "does not call or visit enough." Disgruntled members begin to say things like: "the pastor is not available when I need him," or, "the pastor is too involved with other things, he's really not interested in this church or us." The pastor often has similar feelings; "they say little or nothing to me about my sermons," "they could call me when they have a problem, but they don't," or, "they really don't care about what I do."

As the conflict increases, the tendency is for the pastor and people to withdraw more and more from those with whom they disagree. This is a time when both sides should work harder at communication, because the tendency to withdraw exacerbates the feelings of dissonance.

Decline in Attendance and Giving

During the tenure of the contested pastor, giving and attendance is likely to decline. Some members "lose heart" at being a part of a church consistently engaged in conflict, especially with the pastor. Other members will take weekend trips, or extended vacations, staying away from the church. When the attendance drops, normally the giving decreases, which causes more conflict and fear within the lives of the church leaders.

Special Congregational Factors

Some churches are more prone to conflict because of their history. When conflict is not dealt with properly, there will always be factions disagreeing within the church. If a church has a history of forcing their ministers to leave when conflict arises, it will be much easier to fall into the same pattern rather than sitting down and "reasoning together." Some unhealthy churches experience emotional problems brought by sick individuals and groups who have been in leadership for years. Unless the leadership is replaced, they will always follow the same unhealthy patterns when conflict arises. Where these circumstances exist, the church and pastor need to be on guard, preparing for continuous conflict.

A wise pastor will heed the early warning signs and address them appropriately. Hopefully, a commitment on how to solve the problem and a sense of hope will persist among the leadership and the people. Honest communication must take place. If the warnings are not addressed, the conflict will eventually move to the second stage.

Stage 2 — Dissension and Polarization

During stage two, a new element of shrewdness and calculation enters. The parties begin to call on friends to *discuss* the problem. Many times at this level, the language used to describe the problem moves from specific to general. Offended individuals are alluded to as "some people" as there becomes a need for self-protection. There is a shift from unreserved openness to being guarded. Instead of describing who is doing what, participants report, "We cannot communicate," "There are a lot of problems around here," "A lot of people have hurt feelings," "People should act like Christians around here." Usually, behind each of these generalizations is a factual happening, but those involved want to distance themselves from the other.

At stage two, people are nervous and tension is sensed in the air. They are more guarded in sharing information, fearing that it may be used against them, and indicating a low trust level. Communication is cautious and not clear. Compromise is usually not seen at this level of conflict. People begin to take sides, and an *us against them* attitude begins to be seen.

Stage 3 — Contest of Wills

When conflict reaches stage three, the objective is no longer to solve the problem, but to win. The motive is now to put the opponent "in his proper place." The attitude is "I'm right, so you must be wrong," and "I'm the good person who has the only possible answers." If the pastor does not change to meet their expectations, he must be dismissed.

As I look back on my situation, I wish that I had had the ability to identify the levels of conflict and what to do about it. Looking back, I now realize there were many dynamics that are a part of conflict between the pastor and staff and the pastor and the church leadership. Personality types also play a big part in what happens at each level. There was one person on my staff who believed that because he reacted to something or someone in an emotional way, his feelings could be viewed as "facts." The *actual* facts did not interest him; his mind was made up that the pastor was wrong because his emotions led him to his conclusions.

There were others on the staff and leadership that made general conclusions based on a few isolated facts. They wanted to believe that the pastor had to go, so a case was built upon assumptions and over-generalizations. In level three, generalization takes on an "out of control" quality: "You always," "He never," "Everybody."

People are labeled in stage three. "My side is godly, your side is carnal" is the attitude seen. Scripture is taken out of context and used to prove points. Prayer meetings are held to ask God to remove the *ungodly* person.

In level three, a case is normally built against the person that must lose as they win. As the case is built, the person or persons select only those observations about someone that fits their preconceived conclusion. Normally, the entire case is slanted toward the unfavorable. They refuse to look at the person's good qualities, or his past history as he has been considered successful in the ministry.

Taking sides is another sign that the conflict has shifted to level three. Meetings are held, with groups being told only the information that makes the person look unfavorable. These groups begin to jump to conclusions, and "we must get rid of him" is the underlying theme of the meetings. Speed Leas from the Alban Institute says that this attitude of wanting to get rid of someone is almost always premature because if the causes of the difficulty have not been identified, it is not appropriate to ask for removal of the person or persons without first engaging in a serious effort to remove the causes of the difficulty. Leas explains that while it is understandable that people in pain want to remove the source of the pain, it is not always the case that the pain is caused by an unchangeable person.[1]

I am convinced that even if a request to terminate the pastor comes too soon in the conflict, it is not too late to attempt reconciliation. A good mediator can help the leadership see that they have jumped to conclusions and try to find a resolution before the "divorce" is necessary.

Stage 4 — Factions Solidify

Parties operating at stage four have the objective of hurting their opponents in some way, getting rid of them, or both. Being right and punishing those who are wrong prevails. The behavior differs at stage four from stage three in that changing the other person is no longer enough. Therefore, their only option is the removal of the person from his environment. Examples of stage four conflict include trying to get the pastor fired, attempting to get people to move toward their way of thinking, and away from the pastor's perspective, of trying to get people to leave the church with him.

Clear lines are now marked on who is in which camp, and strong leaders emerge in each group. Rather than concentrating on what's best for the entire church, the subgroup is more concerned about getting their way. The goal is a divorce and hurt.

In my situation, stage four was very hurtful. I had people from the church that decided to tell the leadership of the state where I was pastor, and also served as First Vice President, how terrible I was. A letter writing campaign began to tell state leaders about my problems as a pastor. Letters were sent to our state Executive Director, Church Minister Relation Department, local Director of Missions, and of course, all the leadership in the church. Not one time did the authors of the letter confront me or my wife directly. The intent was to hurt and malign my character as a pastor and leader in the state.

In stage four, members of factions talk about principles more than issues; they talk of truth, trust, God's will, the church's health, and many other biblical-related principles. They bend scripture to their ideas rather than building their ideas to conform to scripture. These principles are used to solidify the group's idea that the ends justify the means.

Other behaviors seen in this stage include detachment from one another so they do not have to see the pain they have caused the other. Unforgiving, cold, self-righteous attitudes prevail during this stage. The parties continue to enlist others that will help them punish or get rid of the bad person. Elaine Herrin Onley in her book *Crying on Sunday, Surviving Forced Termination in Ministry* describes a story that reflects the hurtful attitude seen in stage four. After her husband decided to resign, deacons made the decision to present a unanimous motion to the church to pay a severance package for six months following the forced resignation. When the motion was made to pay the severance package, the pastor and his wife were asked to leave the room. For the next two and one half hours, a debate took place on the floor about taking away the severance package. Even some of the deacons who were part of the "unanimous" decision to give a severance package in the first place now spoke against it. The church voted to take a *love* offering to give to the pastor and his family. Again, the intent was not only to get rid of the pastor, but to hurt him even further by taking away his six-month new start.[2]

There is no middle ground in stage four. The group

with the most power and influence will continue to attack and hurt until they get their desire — a resignation or dismissal. At this level, the choices have crystallized into two: fighting or fleeing. I will share in chapters six and seven suggestions for the pastor when he finds himself in the fight/flight mode.

In my opinion and during my research, I believe that if the conflict reaches stage four, the pastor will have a very difficult time staying and fighting the battle. If the pastor does win the battle to stay, he will find an enormous challenge in leading the church.

Stage 5 — Destroy the Other

Stage five conflict is really a revenge stage. The winning group feels that they must *make the other party pay*. People are not satisfied with a resignation, they want the pastor removed from the face of the earth.[3] Speed Leas says that the final stage is conflict that has run amok.[4] While the objective in stage four is to hurt and get rid of the person, in stage five the objective is to destroy each other. The opposition is seen not only as damaging to the church, but harmful to the community and society in general. An example of stage five is when a pastor resigns, the opposing parties feel obligated to see that the pastor never gets another church position, and obstructs the pastor's search. The opposing parties feel that they cannot stop fighting, because they are helping society and are fighting for God's justice.

I have had countless pastors share with me their grief and hurt concerning what happened after they were forced to resign. It is almost impossible to find a church that will even consider a pastor if he leaves a church without another ministry position. The pastor has given his life through seminary education, serving people, praying, and working endless hours. He feels he is called to be a minister, but must now move into a different direction because of others trying to destroy him. Myra Marshall, in her book *Beyond Termination*, explains that when you talk about the loss of a church position, you are not just talking about a minor element in one's personality. You are talking about a major loss. You are talking about a major restructuring of the personality, separating your church work from your faith in God, and separating your own career — with such heavy identification — from your own relationship to God.[5] Of course, we must realize that we serve a God that is much bigger than the conflict we encounter. This is the only thought that keeps me going.

Regarding these five stages, the first two can be worked through and in the right circumstances, reconciliation can take place. Stage three, reconciliation is much more difficult; by the fourth and fifth stages, reconciliation is impossible.

What is even more difficult to identify is what level each group is working through. One person may be at stage two while the opposing party may be operating from stage four. The person who is working from stage two trying to find a solution or compromise will be overwhelmed when he encounters a group working from stage four. The difference could be compared to the difference between dealing with a house cat vs. a tiger. It is of the highest importance to recognize the type of individual you are dealing with. I have learned that my personality is the type that wants reconciliation, and will attempt to work toward that. I assumed that everyone else operated the same way I did — not true! I have learned through my situation that there are those who do not want reconciliation, but want to hurt you. We must be aware and be as wise as serpents, but gentle as doves.

END NOTES

[1] Speed B. Leas, *Should the Pastor be Fired?* (Washington D.C.: The Alban Institute Inc., 1980), 6-7.

[2] Elaine Herrin Onley, *Crying on Sunday, Surviving Forced Termination in Ministry.* (Macon: Smyth & Helwys Publishing, Inc., 1994) 26.

[3] John Maxwell, *Relationships, A New Beginning or a Bitter End.* (San Diego: Injoy Life Club, 1997) Tape Series Vol. 12 No. 10.

[4] Speed B. Leas, *Moving Your Church Through Conflict.* (Washington D.C.: The Alban Institute Inc., 1985), 22.

[5] Myra Marshall, *Beyond Termination, A Spouses Story of Pain and Healing.* Nashville: Broadman Press, 1990), 59.

CHAPTER SIX

When to Stay and Fight

When you are embroiled in conflict as the leader of the church, you may feel like Job:

"If only my anguish could be weighed and all my misery be placed on the scales! It would surely outweigh the sand of the sea." (Job 6:2-3).

Experiencing attacks from people can crush your spirit, diminish your sense of personhood and self-worth, and even threaten your attachment to the church. You may have a spectrum of feelings ranging from anger, frustration, confusion, and depression to fatigue, tension, and total discouragement. These feelings might lead you to wonder, "What am I doing here? Should I leave or stay?"[1] During conflict in the church one of the most difficult decisions a pastor must make is: "Should I stay and fight, or do I resign my position?"

The question to stay or leave is not a question to be answered without first going to God in prayer and asking Him to lead you through the decision. Jesus Christ gives us the secret for our lives and ministry. *Truly, truly I say to you, the Son can do nothing of Himself* (John 5:19a). How many times have I tried to do something alone, winging it! Yet Jesus tells us that even he can do nothing alone: for *whatever the Father does, these things the Son also does in like manner (v. 19b)*. With emphasis, he continues, *I can do nothing on My own initiative ... but the Father abiding in Me does His works (John 5:30a; 14:10b)*. We must allow God to give us wisdom and discernment as we swim through the murky waters of church conflict.

After experiencing the difficulty of leaving a church, I have prayed, interviewed pastors who have chosen to stay and many who have made the choice to resign. In chapter seven I will give reasons to resign.

Listed below are several reasons to stay and fight. Test them against your perception of God's will for you, your family, and the church.

When the Pastor's Attitude is to Minister to the Congregation

There is a prevailing attitude of pastors who resist a move toward termination. "It's not fair," "My ministry is not complete here," "They can't do this to me," "I haven't done anything to deserve this," "I've done everything *not* to deserve this — I have given my life to this church, I have worked endless hours, I have counseled people, performed weddings, funerals and baby dedications. I have visited the hospitals, I visited those who were sick and depressed, now they want to get rid of me after I have given so much." The pastor must ask the question, "Do I love these people enough to genuinely minister to their needs?" Pastor, can you get past the hurt and resentment to serve even those who have been the most vocal against you? I am convinced that if a pastor can feel good about being with the people, if he wants to continue living in the same ministry area, and wants to support the congregation, (all of them) in their times of trouble, then the motivation is appropriate for staying.

In my research I have found that most clergy who resist leaving do it for reasons not relevant to the question of ministering to the people. Resistance is based on arguments such as: "This isn't fair," I'm not going to let those #^?%*#\^* people tell me what to do and push me around," "My kids are not out of high school yet," "This will keep me from getting another ministry position," and many other reasons.

If the pastor wants to be with the congregation and work through ways to rebuild relationships so that support, personal counseling, and genuine caring can take place then it's all right to resist. This is definitely not an easy approach, and some will continue to be hostile.

When the Adversity Comes
From a Small Minority

When a pastor wants to be with a group of people, I am referring to the vast majority of them. When there is a small minority in the church who are trying to "run off the pastor," and this group does not have the support or sympathy of the majority of the congregation, then there is cause to resist. The problem I encountered, and many pastors encounter, is that the congregation is misread with regard to how supportive the members are of our ministry and us. When you hear the complaints day after day from the minority, it begins to wear you down and you begin to believe there are many who are dissatisfied, especially if you are told "there are many people who want you to leave."

Many pastors have shared with me that the dissension normally begins with one person that does not like the pastor or a member of his family. The unhappy person then begins a campaign to get rid of the pastor. Sadly, there are very few lay people that will follow biblical guidelines and ask the one person to keep quiet. One pastor from Missouri shared with me about one lady that began a campaign that eventually led him to resign under pressure. The pastor shared the plan of salvation with a lady that was living with a man and not married. The young lady accepted Christ and attended the church, allowing the pastor to baptize her. The antagonist, a Sunday school teacher, made a statement in an adult Sunday School class that the church should not allow "sinners" to join the church. The pastor, as he sat in the class shared with the class that the church is the very place that "sinners" should attend. The teacher yelled at the pastor, throwing her Bible on the floor. From that moment the antagonist used her influence to create such difficulty for the pastor, he eventually resigned.

As long as churches allow one or two unhappy members lead campaigns to get rid of pastors many churches will not grow spiritually or numerically. My prayer is that there will be laymen who wake up and begin following scriptural guidelines, especially as they relate to their spiritual leader.

When a Pattern Must Be Broken

Forced terminations are seen most in churches that have a pattern of firing or forcing their pastors to leave. As I mentioned earlier, I am the third pastor in a row forced to terminate my position as senior pastor. I spoke to one of my predecessors who actually named the same three men that worked behind the scenes in both of our forced terminations. Apparently, when a difficulty arises, instead of working through the problem, it's easier to get rid of the pastor especially if that's the pattern.

If the pastor is healthy, he might find it wise to resist overtures that he resign if there is a definite pattern that must be broken. In many churches the majority of the people are so uncomfortable with conflict and so reticent about-facing it that they would prefer to accommodate to dissent rather than seriously explore whether or not the proposals being made are in the best interest of the church. A pastor may do well to say no to the dissidents and yes to an open exploration of the issues being raised, looking for ways to see what changes can be made — short of changing pastors.

When You Feel Healthy Enough
To Work Through The Conflict

Dealing with conflict on a daily basis can have an adverse effect on your health, and the health of your family. We are rightfully fearful of conflict. We well know its potential to hurt others as well as ourselves.[2] If you make a decision to stay and try to work through the conflict I suggest that you get with a doctor and make sure your health is in order and you do not have signs of burnout. *See the Appendix for a burnout test.*

I encourage you not to resign prematurely. I know too many pastors who precipitously resign because of an antagonist when it was neither necessary nor helpful. Resigning prematurely can hinder God's mission and ministry in your life and in the church where you pastor.

I do not deny that some situations will call for resignation, which will be covered in chapter seven. I myself feel that I had to resign or I would have had a major health breakdown.

Seriously consider hanging in there as you pray and ask God's direction. When a pastor relinquishes his position, the solution is often temporary. When the new replacement arrives, the problem begins again. Also, when you as a pastor go to another church, normally there are problems there, which have not been taken care of. If you are dealing with a difficult person in your church remember that the antagonist's continuing aggressive behavior originates within him- or herself; you just happened to be the most convenient target at the time.[3] Keep in mind, your resignation can allow the antagonist to feel reinforced and become more powerful in the congregation. The next pastor will have a very difficult person to deal with.

The pastor rarely experiences 100% support from the congregation. It's difficult to stay as pastor when you think others are against you. We all want to be liked and appreciated, but human nature does not allow such luxury. Consider the following statistics: According to the Gallup polls, one of the most popular presidents in American history was Franklin Roosevelt, who, at the peak of his popularity in January, 1942, had 84 percent of the citizens' support. This means that 16 percent were *not* in agreement with his politics and practices. Most presidents have received 40-60 percent support as a rule; for some, public support has sunk far lower at times. Even presidents with less than 30 percent support did not resign. No one has 100 percent of the people 100 percent of the time.[4] Pastor, do not let the lack of complete support hurt your self-image. You probably have more support than you realize. In actuality, the vocal minority is still a minority, despite their intensity. As Ulysses S. Grant said, "There are always more of them until they are counted."

Before you resign, keep in mind that you must be God directed, rather than depending exclusively on feedback from others. If you only look to others to validate who you are, you will eventually run into problems. Let God lead.

END NOTES

[1] Kenneth C. Haugk, *Antagonists in the Church: How to Identify and Deal with Destructive Conflict.* (Minneapolis: Augsburg Publishing House, 1988), 173.

[2] Keith Huttenlocker, *Conflict and caring,* (Grand Rapids: Zondervan Publishing House, 1988), 7.

[3] Haugk, *Antagonists in the Church*, 174.

[4] Ibid., 175.

CHAPTER SEVEN

When to Resign

Resignation is usually unnecessary, but there are times that the best decision for the pastor, his family and the church is to resign. To leave without another position in ministry is very threatening creating anxiety and fear. For many ministers the idea of leaving is a relief that overrides the anxiety and fear.

I made the decision that resigning would put me in control of my life and future not allowing the deacons to control me any longer. I wanted to leave with dignity and my head held high. Terminating a ministry position is similar to a terminally ill person that knows they will die soon. Terminally ill people have four major tasks to perform when they discover they will die soon:

1) They need to take control of what remains of their life (as far as possible), with some help if necessary, as opposed to passively letting others dictate the way they will die.

2) They need to get their affairs in order (make a will if they haven't already done so, take care of loans, debts, etc,).

3) They need to let old grudges go. This implies dealing directly and candidly with those against whom

they harbor resentment, anger, disappointment, etc,

4) They need to say, "thank you" to the people whom they feel gratitude.[1]

It's very difficult to make a decision to resign, especially under pressure. Here are a few reasons for resignation that I suggest you pray through and evaluate how this will effect your family and the church where you pastor.

When the Holy Spirit Tells You to Leave

Pastor, when you truly spend time in prayer and seek the leadership of the Holy Spirit, I am convinced that He will let you know when it is time to leave your ministry position. Even though the circumstances are difficult and your emotions are shattered, God still loves you and has a plan for your life. I remember that I continued to try to work things out even though there was opposition against me. I did not want to let my position go because of fear; the fear of lost income, not being able to pastor again, the fear of what my colleagues would say about me, and many other fears.

The night before I resigned, as I was meeting with the deacons, several of the men decided to tell me everything they could think of that was wrong with me. It was difficult to listen to, but God used the time to speak to me. I sensed the Holy Spirit saying, "you needed to hear this to realize that your ministry is completed here, I am now releasing you." I was able to go home and explain to my family that I was going to resign as pastor.

When there is Loss of Trust and Respect
by the Majority

Another cause of involuntary terminations comes when the *majority* of the congregation does not believe that a pastor's proclamations approximate his life-style or behavior.[2] Should the majority of the congregation believe that the pastor reveals information given in confidence, should the people believe that the pastor is not fulfilling his previously agreed upon job description, should they believe the pastor is misusing church funds, or should the people believe the pastor does not genuinely like and respect them — there exists a situation in which the trust relationship has broken down.

Pastor, even though you may be primarily right, continuing to function in your position as leader becomes difficult at best when most of the members of the church have lined up against you. If you stay your effectiveness as pastor will be very difficult. Resignation is certainly appropriate in this instance.

There are times that pastors feel that standards of behavior are asked of him that are not kept by those demanding a certain lifestyle. Yes, a pastor must live at a standard that is seen by most as a higher standard. There are standards that church members must live by as directed by God's Word. When church members tell lies, gossip, and work behind the scene to get rid of a pastor, it is difficult for the pastor to respect those members. Recently I spoke with a pastor from Missouri who was serving at his first full time church when a few members decided that he must leave. The chairman of deacons told the pastor that his terminally ill father did not want the pastor to visit him in the hospital again.

Confused, the young pastor decided to follow the wishes of the elderly gentleman. In a business meeting it was said that the pastor responded to the request; "If the man does not want to see me again, he might as well just die." Of course the pastor did not say anything negative about the man, but a lie was told and people believed it. This pastor who eventually resigned still has a difficult time with the chairman of deacons who lied about him.

It is difficult to know if the majority of the congregation has lost respect for the pastor, but if the pastor senses this is the case, he may want to make plans to leave. There are times that bringing in a mediator can help evaluate the climate of the church, which will give the pastor an indication about the feelings of the congregation concerning his credibility.

When Staying Will Harm the Church

Deciding to vacate your position also involves questions of moral responsibility. Being a church leader involves certain responsibilities to the people you serve. If staying, as pastor will cause the church to split right down the middle, you as the leader must be responsible to God.

Even if you weathered the storm and came through with the majority of support, resignation may be the expedient and caring action. Your presence might simply be an unpleasant reminder of that time of strife. I do caution you as pastor not to give up too soon. Time will tell if you suffered a permanent loss of effectiveness. If the difficulty increases over a period of time, then perhaps you should move on.

You should consider resigning if as pastor you have

made serious mistakes or committed actual offenses that could create a scandal or offense, if so, then moving on might be the only self-respecting course of action. Again, think of the body of Christ and how they will be affected.

When Staying has an Adverse Effect on You and Your Family

Consider leaving when staying poses a risk to your physical or emotional health. If the major stress you are experiencing comes from the difficulty as serving as pastor in a hostile environment there could be adverse effects on you and your health. One of the main reasons that I chose to resign was because of many health problems due to years of dealing with conflict, which caused stress. I was experiencing hypertension, my immune system was very weak which allowed for sickness.

As I look back, and with the help of a wonderful Christian counselor I had to admit that I was in denial concerning burnout. If I did not resign I do believe I would have experienced a serious health problem.

As mentioned in chapter three, burnout is a major cause of forced terminations. Let me explain further. Brooks Faulkner in his book, *Burnout in Ministry,* shares danger signals of burnout in the physical life of the minister:

1) He begins to feel tired frequently;
2) He begins to gain weight;
3) He spends fewer hours at previously favorite activities;
4) His sexual energies have waned;
5) He begins to lose weight;
6) He finds himself more dependent on stimulants

and / or sedatives;
7) He exercises when the urge hits, but it hits infrequently;
8) He takes on fewer and fewer responsibilities;
9) He places high value on making it on less rest;
10) He begins to carry a constant comrade: exhaustion;
11) He begins to live with full-time vulnerability;[3]

Not all these symptoms will be seen in the minister, he cannot gain and lose weight at the same time, but if the minister is experiencing three or more of the symptoms, he is probably experiencing stress and burnout in his life. I was experiencing at least eight of the symptoms when I resigned as pastor. I did not recognize it at the time since I was in denial. As I look back and review the list of symptoms, I am glad that I made the decision to resign and work through a healing process.

The pastor's family may also experience symptoms of stress. As I interviewed pastors who were forced to terminate, I heard many stories concerning the stress load on their wives and children. One pastor shared with me that his thirteen-year-old daughter had the youth in the church act rudely to her because of the conflict with a few members and the pastor. Three years later, the daughter now sixteen says that she will never attend church again in her life. What a tragedy. Pastor, please consider your family and their feelings, especially if you decide to stay and fight.

How to Resign
When you have considered the factors in this chap-

ter, and resignation seems proper to you, here are some possible ways on how to resign:

Prepare a written statement that is honest. I suggest that you stick to the facts and not editorialize on each statement. When I resigned, I shared with the people about stress and exhaustion. I also shared with them that my decision to resign was for the well being of the church.

Leave with dignity. I suggest that when you read your letter of resignation hold your head high and look into the eyes of the people. Don't stoop to the level of name-calling or mud slinging.

Apologize sincerely if, in any way, you are to blame for what happened. Ask forgiveness from those you may have offended. This can be done before the congregation or committee or board. In short, apologize before the appropriate people.

Ask the congregation to remember you at your best. There are many things ministers do to help the congregation. Ask them to remember the times of personal ministry rather than one event that may have led to a resignation.

Resignation is never an easy choice; it calls for a great deal of prayer, thought and personal struggle.

END NOTES
[1] Roy M. Oswald, *Running Through The Thistles, Terminating a Ministerial Relationship With a Parish*, (Washington D.C.: The Alban Institute, Inc., 1978), 6-7.
[2] Speed B. Leas, *Should the Pastor be Fired?* Washington D.C.: The Alban Institute, Inc., 1980), 11.
[3] Brooks R. Faulkner, *Burnout in Ministry*, (Nashville: Broadman Press, 1981), 64-65.

CHAPTER EIGHT

How to Deal with Conflict

Dealing with conflict and confrontation is one of the most important skills you can learn. Most of us do not like to deal with conflict; we are scared of letting others know what we really think because we fear that they will use what we say against us. We even believe that our honesty will hurt others, so we avoid confrontation or put on a strong front.

The word *conflict* comes from the Latin word *conflictus,* which literally means, "a striking together." The striking together could be between two or more forces, persons or groups. There are basically three types of conflict; interpersonal conflict, intrapersonal conflict, and substantive conflict.

Interpersonal conflict is conflict between persons; this can be two persons or a number of persons. Interpersonal conflict is normally not based on differences over issues, but what one person thinks or feels about the other person or group.

Intrapersonal conflict is strife within a person. This type of conflict refers to the feelings of confusion, frustration, unrest and even guilt that we feel within ourselves. With our inner self in turmoil, it may be easy to displace this frustration on others to ease our personal pain.

Substantive conflict is friction over issues. This type of conflict grows out of differences about methods, values and goals. Especially in a church setting we see substantive conflict because there are so many people who have varied ideas about the direction of the church. A good leader is one that has the ability to cast a vision and have people feel as though they are part of that vision.

The problem in church conflict is that one cannot neatly sort out substantive conflict from interpersonal conflict situations. Most conflicts begin with substantive issues and then develop into interpersonal strife. On the other hand, interpersonal conflict can quickly lead to the discovery of issues that influence confrontation.

In this chapter I am sharing from experience how to deal with conflict and hopefully help pastors and churches avoid a forced termination.

Identify Your Conflict Style

We all have a conflict management style; it can range from aggressive confrontation to completely passive avoidance. We develop survival responses that are acted out, especially in threatening situations. Corporate psychologists have labeled these responses with animal names — for the solutions they seek.

Sharks — "I win; you lose"

Sharks tend to be competitive and aggressive, with the only solution to a problem being the one they want. Sharks use intimidation, power, persuasion, and even threats to get their way. They are not particularly interested in cooperating with other people, but instead approach conflict in a very forceful way. The rationale is normally: "I don't care what other people think. I'm going to make sure I get my own way."

A typical shark response in a church setting is when the attacker waits until a business meeting, and then tries to embarrass the pastor by stating things that should have been dealt with privately. Another shark response is to get others to agree with them using whatever means available and trying to rally hostility against the pastor or whatever person or group they are against. It is dangerous to always give sharks their way. When sharks are allowed to rule the church, anger builds in others as they feel coerced, and a precarious dependency on the strong-willed individual can develop.

A pastor that uses shark-like aggressiveness will use the pulpit to attack people who he feels are against him. Normally, his sermons will be laced with animosity and ridicule.

Foxes — "Everyone wins a little and loses a little"

Foxes are flexible, and they want compromise. They like to work behind the scene trying to negotiate both parties to accept their solution. Compromise usually occurs on a more superficial level; you give up something, the other person gives up something, and eventually you come to a resolution. Sometimes a compromise is what is needed, but it is not always the answer. It can leave people half-satisfied and half-committed to the solution. Many times, the problem that was compromised upon will emerge later in a different form.

Turtles — "I withdraw"

Turtles are so frightened by conflict; they pull back,

avoid and circumvent any conflict situation. They can only survive when there is no conflict, so they flee any dispute. Some will actually get up and walk out of a room when conflict begins to take place. Others will withdraw emotionally.

At times, avoiding conflict is the right thing to do. In fact, Proverbs reminds us it is the glory of a person to overlook an insult. We need to choose our battles carefully.

Turtles appear to be peaceful and even gentle, but deep inside they are hiding anger and frustration. By pulling into a shell as a way of dealing with conflict, the anger and frustration will continue.

Teddy Bears — *"I'll lose so you can win"*

When dealing with confrontation, teddy bears readily concede their own interests to oblige the disagreeing person. The teddy bear will placate the shark. They want to keep peace at almost any price. The teddy bear will show great concern for others, trying to create a loving atmosphere. They attempt to accept responsibility for the problem in a sacrificial fashion, which can be seen by some as super-spiritual.

Owls — *"Let's find a way for everyone to win"*

The owls look for ways that are beneficial to everyone. They want to see everyone leave the room with a win-win solution. They collaborate with all parties involved until they arrive at a mutually satisfying resolution. Owls are willing to stay with the task until the difficulty is solved. Collaborators take advantage of conflict, seeing it as an opportunity to strengthen a group, not destroy it.

When you choose to collaborate, you get actively involved in working out the conflict by asserting what you want, while still trying to cooperate with others. When you take the time to listen to each other's wants and discover the underlying needs you can begin to work toward a win-win situation.

Deal with Conflict Immediately

Many people's response to conflict is to give in, give up, or ignore the situation and pretend nothing is wrong. Often we think, "If I just ignore the problem, it might go away." In reality, most problems that require confrontation do not go away. They are like infections: if we ignore them, they can spread. Soon, that terrible pain gets worse and can even turn into blood poisoning.

Sometimes we avoid conflict because we have lost hope of improving the situation. "It wouldn't do any good," we reply to those who urge us to take action. There is truly a price in avoiding conflict. Integrity is lost. Our self-respect suffers when we allow ourselves to be treated in an unfavorable way, and pretend the treatment is acceptable. Conflict avoidance tends to preclude any chance of making the situation better. Old practices from others remain, failure and futility are unchallenged, and the pain lingers, and wrongs reign.

I have learned that the best time to handle conflict is before it arises. In dealing with certain staff, I allowed wrong behavior to continue, believing that I was giving them a second chance. I would overlook untruths being told, financial discrepancies, and meetings being held to persuade people to join their camp. By not dealing immediately with the problem staff members, they were able to persuade several influential people to follow them.

As we follow the Biblical principles laid out in Matthew 18, we must confront the person we are experiencing conflict with. When done properly, the conflict can normally be taken care of immediately instead of allowing time to amplify the problem.

We must continue to confront — wisely, directly, humbly. Loving confrontation helps people grow in Christ; ultimately, it spares them much pain.

Set Clear Ground Rules

As I have interviewed pastors concerning their forced terminations, I have discovered that many of them never knew what the rules were. There were no clear guidelines that were followed, and many of the pastors were left in the dark. I suggest that you provide some type of structure that is agreed upon by the pastor and the church leadership. Here are a few suggestions:

- *Who is invited to what meetings.* In my case, there were several meetings that took place without my knowledge. Secret meetings are usually a strategy for building a case. Like me, most ministers are highly threatened by secret meetings. The church owes the minister the diplomacy and dignity of being straight. The pastor should know in advance who would be at the meetings. Most pastors that I interviewed were thrown into a situation where several boards had gotten together several times without the pastor, the decision was already made, then the pastor was brought in to face many people. Again in my case, the last meeting I was allowed to be a part of involved me as the pastor facing the deacon body, the personnel committee, the staff, and even the support staff. Several days of meetings had gone on prior to my entrance. When I walked in, I felt so alone and apprehensive because of such a large crowd. I wish that I had had a list of who would be present in the meeting; if so, I could have prepared myself.

- *What the agenda will be at each meeting.* Every participant needs to know in advance what the agenda will be. It is only fair that each person in the meetings should have the opportunity to prepare through meditation and prayer. Many pastors reported to me that they did not have an agenda, allowing each person to simply vent their dislike or frustration toward the pastor. A clear outlined agenda should be agreed upon by the church leadership and pastor prior to the meeting explaining that there will be no other items discussed at that particular meeting.

- *Establish a stopping time.* Prior to the meeting, a stopping time should be agreed upon by all parties involved. Sometimes matters that are sensitive in nature may need to have two or more meetings, allowing time for prayer and processing between the meetings. Rarely are sensitive issues dealt with honestly in one meeting. Also, if meetings are extra long many people, because of exhaustion and mental fatigue, will make the wrong decision. Setting an agreed-upon stopping time (and sticking to it) will avoid panic on either side. It also avoids having people become so emotionally entangled that the perspective of a possible solution is lost.

- *Give both sides equal time in expressing views.* Again, when there are secret meetings held and charges are made against the pastor, many people begin to believe the charges and they process them as fact. By the time the pastor has the opportunity to defend himself against the charges, many do not want to listen — they have heard the charges over and over again, and from different angles. Each side should have equal time in sharing their views. I believe that when charges are raised against the pastor, he should have the opportunity to defend himself immediately. One minister shared with a group in a workshop for forced-terminated pastors that he went to another state for a two-week vacation. Upon his return, he was met by the chairman of deacons at the parsonage. He explained to the pastor that the deacons had met immediately after he left, and voted to request his resignation. On the following Wednesday night, the church was informed that there would be a vote taken concerning the pastor immediately following the Sunday service. (This was a procedure called upon by the church's constitution and by-laws). The church voted a two-thirds majority for his termination. When the pastor asked what the charges were, he was informed that three years was long enough in any church, and he did not visit the church members enough. When the pastor asked why he did not have the opportunity to respond to the charges, the deacon said "the church felt it would be best for all if the matter was not discussed with the pastor until action was taken." As a human being, the pastor should have had the right to be heard before any vote was taken.

- *Agree to treat each other with respect.* I am referring to listening to each other without interruption, and agreeing not to get angry or express hostility, even if one disagrees with something being said. Most of all, it is important to agree that you will try to see each other's point of view.

Once you have laid down ground rules, you can always refer to them later, especially if the process breaks down or tempers begin to flare. If a breakdown does take place, it's a signal to call time out, and refocus everyone back to the ground rules.

For the best results, make sure that you get everyone's agreement when you set the rules, as well as his or her suggestions for additional rules. It should be easy to agree here since you are merely suggesting rules of customary human courtesy and respect. If you cannot seem to agree on a set of rules, take that as a sign that the feelings underlying the conflict may be running too deep to deal with the difficulty at that time.

Allow for Hope that a Mutually Satisfying Solution Will Be Found

Once you decide a conflict is worth resolving without avoiding the matter, conceding to what someone else wants, or forcing through your own ideas because you have the power to do so, you are left with negotiating.

The two ways of negotiating are through collaboration or compromise. The two approaches are similar in involving some give and take. The major difference is that compromise centers on surface issues, and collaboration tries to go deeper.

In compromise, both parties share at the beginning what they want and hope to receive at the end of the meeting. As the discussion continues, each side will begin to make concessions and counter-offers until both parties can agree on the outcome.

When you decide to collaborate, you go beyond the initial positions to look at the underlying needs and concerns of both parties. Collaboration takes more time and energy since each person shares their deeper concerns. A good example of collaboration is when a staff person continues to arrive late, which causes a conflict with the pastor. The lateness may possibly be the difficulty of the staff person to manage his or her time properly, or the underlying, deeper conflict may be dissatisfaction with the ministry position. He or she may feel lack of respect or an acknowledgement of what they accomplish and they are responding by disconnection from the pastor or staff. If only the surface issue is dealt with, the pastor may say; "start coming to work on time or you will be reprimanded." This superficial treatment is not likely to have a long-term effect, because the root of the problem still remains. The staff person may come to work on time, but there will be problems later. By contrast, using collaboration encourages each person to bring his or her real needs and desires in the open. The observant pastor will question the staff person and allow openness for an honest response without fear. When the issues are brought to the table the pastor can then make some changes to allow for acknowledgement given to the staff person.

You might know that you want to work toward a win-win outcome. Which method is the best for the conflict you are in; compromise or collaboration? The key of course, is to be aware of the specific circumstances that surround the conflict and remain flexible as you negotiate. Gini Graham Scott in her book; *Resolving Conflict*[1] helps distinguish between those situations where compromise is especially useful and those where collaboration may be best.

Choose Compromise when:
- the issues are relatively simple and clear cut
- there isn't much time to reach a solution or you want to achieve a resolution as quickly as possible
- it would be better to achieve a temporary agreement quickly, and then deal with the more serious or underlying issues later
- you and the other party (or parties) to the negotiation aren't that concerned about the goals or outcome of conflict
- you haven't been able to resolve the matter using collaboration or you haven't been able to get your way by using your own power to force a solution

Choose collaboration when:
- the issues are fairly complex and require a detailed discussion to work out a solution acceptable to both
- both parties are willing to spend the time needed to deal with the underlying needs and concerns

- both parties feel their concerns are very important and don't want to compromise them
- both parties are willing to be open-minded and approach the negotiation in a spirit of good faith, which includes being willing to listen and understand the other's concerns
- both parties want to achieve a permanent agreement, rather than a quick temporary solution, and are willing to deal with the issue now

If you are involved in a conflict where negotiation seems suitable, the key is to look beneath the surface and find what the real wants and needs are. You may find that some of the wants and needs of yourself or others may not be very admirable. Some underlying wants may be ambition to move up, a desire to hurt another individual, or other wrong reasons for conflict. If you find yourself in a situation where negative emotions are brought to the surface, a third party should be brought in to help with the negotiations.

Conflict Management

Conflict management is an attempt to coexist with a problem or with problem persons through intentional devices that maintain the conflict with acceptable limits.[2] When a person avoids conflict, he can feel like a powerless victim of the circumstance. Conflict management takes some limited control over the difficulty. Conflict management is active, not passive. It is what we have to settle for when conflict resolution is not possible. Conflict management is the attempt to live with the problem, since resolution for the moment is not possible.

Agreeing to disagree and attempting dialogue are the main ingredients of conflict management. A man who is now in leadership in a state convention told me of a time when he was an associate pastor of a large church and difficulty began to take place between he and the pastor. Over a period of time the associate tried to work through the conflict with his pastor. He began to realize that resolution of the problem would not be an option, so he approached the pastor and explained that he would leave the position, asking the pastor to give him time to find another position and relocate. The two men were able to manage the conflict with integrity and even preserve some intimacy. The associate was able to find another position in three months. This is possible because conflict management denies neither the reality of the problem nor one's feelings about it, but enables both parties to work through to some type of conclusion with integrity.

Conflict management is usually a tentative arrangement, since with an ongoing problem it is always possible that the truce will be broken. Our tolerance for conflict management is limited, prompting us to take action eventually, whether wise or unwise. Yet we should make no apology for conflict management when it is the best we can do under the circumstances.

END NOTES

1 Gini Graham Scott, *Resolving Conflict*, (Oakland: New Harbinger Publications, 1990), 158-159.

2 Keith Huttenlocker, *Conflict and Caring*. (Grand Rapids: Zondervan Publishing House, 1988), 31.

3 Ibid., 33.

CHAPTER NINE

Practical Suggestions for the Pastor Facing a Forced Termination

When I went through my forced termination, I wish that someone could have given my family and me some guidance. There were several circumstances that we allowed to take place because we trusted certain individuals, and now realize that they were not thinking of our best interest. Here are some practical suggestions from a pastor who has been there.

Listen and Learn

When a pastor faces a forced termination it's difficult to learn about ourselves, but as we go through difficulty we can evaluate what type of person we are. As I discussed in chapter eight, there are basically five different conflict management styles. Allow the conflict that you are in to help evaluate what style of conflict management you possess. If you always avoid conflict, I suggest you work toward changing your conflict management style. Conflict is inevitable, especially if you are going to serve in a church. You must work toward being a person that works toward the best possible conflict solution. I now work more directly with conflict, trying to handle it immediately.

As you face a forced termination are you trusting in

God? It's easy to point fingers and shout accusations toward our attackers. In fact, we can get so engrossed in the problem that we can forget that God is still in control. Trust God to guide you through the feelings you are experiencing. Cry out to God; tell Him how you feel. If you feel persecuted, angry, hostile — tell God in prayer. Allow the Holy Spirit to comfort and guide you as you work through the difficulty.

If there is a pattern of being forced to terminate, look at your interpersonal skills. Maybe there are areas in your life that need to be changed especially in how you react to people. Allow God to work on your heart as He continues to mold and change you into the image of Jesus Christ. As we listen, we can learn so much about ourselves. Evaluate what you hear and make changes where changes need to be made.

What if Offered a "Leave of Absence?"

It is difficult to determine if a "leave of absence" is appropriate for the pastor who is facing a forced termination. In some cases a "leave of absence" might help resolve some kinds of tension that are between the pastor and the church leadership. If the pastor's health is in danger a "leave of absence" can be a positive experience for the pastor to take time to regain his health.

The danger of taking a "leave of absence" is that it can be a time for those who want the pastor to leave, to begin influencing church members to oppose the pastor. If the pastor is not present to defend himself, it is easier to get people to believe whatever charges are being brought against the minister.

In my case, I should not have taken a "leave of absence" because many of the staff used the time to recruit and continue working against me. The church even allowed the assistant pastor, who wanted to be the pastor, to preach each week in my absence. A few months after my resignation, he became the pastor.

If you feel that the time away will be used against you, I strongly urge you not to take a "leave of absence." If your health is in jeopardy, a "leave of absence" may be the time away you need to restore your health.

Bring in a Personal Representative for the Pastor

Much has been written about a consultant, mediator, or referee for churches and pastors experiencing conflict, but I have never heard anything said about having a personal representative for the pastor who is being forced to terminate. When a pastor is being forced to terminate he becomes so emotionally, physically and mentally drained that it's difficult to perform even simple tasks. Your mental state is so strained that it's troublesome to even make decisions. There were times that I was in meetings; exhausted from lack of sleep and a proper diet I didn't even know how to answer questions with a clear thought. I feel that I was taken advantage of during this time because of my mental, emotional and physical state of being. I needed a personal representative that could help me think through the process that I was experiencing. I suggest that if you do not have a close friend that is a pastor who could be your personal representative, hire an attorney to help you work through the difficult process of being forced to terminate.

What about a Severance Package?

If you are forced to terminate your position as pastor, it is customary to receive a severance package or continued salary. Speed Leas from The Alban Institute explains that there are several factors that should be taken into account when a severance package is being considered:

- How long has the pastor served the church?
- What are the prospects of the pastor finding another congregation?
- How long will the job search take?
- Is a career change for the pastor probable?
- What is the ability of the congregation to help financially with the transition?

Sad to say, some churches appear to express their anger through some forms of financial punishment. Other churches seem much more generous. Churches must keep in mind that pastors when forced to terminate are normally not in their hometown where their family members could support them. Also, it's very difficult for a pastor to be accepted by another congregation when they are not presently serving in a church.

Most ministers do not benefit from the unemployment funds provided by most businesses. The Employment Security Commission and the state Insurance Commission have not been cooperative in working out a possible unemployment program for ministers. The reasons are valid. They feel the churches and the denomination need their own program.[1] The sad thing is that most conventions do not have unemployment payments for their ministers. Some states have been able to "rescue" some families who have been forced to terminate without a severance package, but it's very short-term.

Consequently, the burden of the provisions needed rests upon the churches where the ministers serve. Churches should set guidelines prior to a pastor coming that states what a severance package looks like if the minister is forced to terminate. Some of my colleagues would say that setting in advance a severance package is making plans to fail. I feel that if the minister knows what a severance package is, he will be able to minister in a more secure environment. I spoke with one pastor that had been forced to terminate and the church voted to give him a severance package, but in the next month's business meeting took the package back. The pastor and his family were devastated and very hurt. When he was called at his next church he shared what had happened to him, the result was the church wanting their pastor to feel secure, voted that if he was ever forced to leave he would receive a continued salary for one year. The church even changed the constitution and by-laws stating that this decision would never be changed. The pastor explained to me that the decision gave him protection and he was able to minister in a greater way. As of this time he has successfully served as pastor for over seven years.

In my research of pastors being forced to terminate, it takes many months to find new employment, therefore, I say to pastors and churches alike; be fair in the severance financial package.

Pastor, make sure that when you receive a severance package, the money is given up front. In my case I was given a check weekly over a designated period of time, but to receive the checks I had to meet monthly with two of the church leaders. They felt free to ask questions about my personal life and family which I resented.

END NOTES
[1] Brooks R. Faulkner, Forced Termination, (Nashville: Broadman Press, 1986), 88.

CHAPTER TEN

Dealing with Anger Produced by a Forced Termination

Most of us find ourselves exploding from time to time and then regretting it later. The explosions occur because we don't like to be angry and we try to keep it on the inside. Anger is a lot like a pressure cooker. We can only suppress it for so long, it eventually erupts. If you don't blow, like an overheated pressure cooker, you may have an internal explosion. This usually means self-hatred, depression, major illness or all the above.

Unresolved anger is that videotape of past offenses that keeps playing over and over in our minds, doing incredible damage to us and everyone around us. Gary Smalley gives a great illustration of anger in his conferences. He says we should think of anger as a sticky, bad-smelling, dangerous substance than can be compressed and stuffed into something like a spray can. Different people have different-sized cans - and different degrees of compression - depending on how much anger they're carrying and for how long.

What happens? Angry people tend to go around spraying their anger on other people. The spray is felt by others as meanness, insensitivity, negativity, and general offenses, and the "sprayers" may not even realize how they're behaving or how it affects other people. They just keep spraying in every direction everywhere like skunks that constantly feel threatened. And anger spray stings like an acid that burns.

There are several consequences of unresolved anger; we distance ourselves from others, God, even ourselves. Anger has the power to keep us miserable. It can imprison us, bind us and make us miserable to live with.

When a pastor is fired or forced to resign, anger is a definite result. Your source of income has been removed, you are embarrassed in front of your family and friends, and your whole emotional life has been thrown into upheaval. The problem in the ministry is that pastors are told that they cannot show anger, therefore many pastors turn anger inward, which results in depression. What you must avoid is keeping this anger inside. Not only will it eat away at you; it will also be transparent to potential future church members or employers.

Anger is a powerful emotional process that affects us at different times for different reasons. Anger, as with all emotions, comes from within. It is a normal reaction we have to something or someone. We must learn to express our anger in appropriate ways. Anger is a feeling of displeasure resulting in injury, mistreatment, opposition, etc., and usually showing itself in a desire to fight back at the supposed cause of this feeling.

The cause or source of our anger will determine how we experience the anger process. Little things may not create a strong reaction of anger. However, a series of little things on a stressful day may cause us to get mad enough to fight back verbally or physically. Usually, the more important the issue, the more intense our anger response will be.

It is important for each of us to note sources of our individual anger, no matter how big or small they seem to us. An anger stimulus for one person may not generate an anger response for others. In addition, our reactions may change over time as we grow, develop, and learn through experiences in our lives.

Anger demands a response.

Make a mental note of how angry you get. Ask yourself, "Am I just a little ticked, or am I *really* angry?" This question must be asked quickly when you experience an anger stimulus. Realizing the degree of your anger will help you to understand your possible responses. With practice, everyone can accurately assess his or her anger responses. The words we use to describe our anger like *annoyed* or *furious*, can be clues. If you can understand your responses to anger, then you can learn to work with your behavior in healthy ways by choosing an appropriate response.

There are constructive and destructive ways to handle anger. Anger can be directed toward oneself, other people, or to objects. Anger directed at oneself is most likely to be destructive.

Outward signs of anger toward self may be actions that hurt the person. For example, an individual who is angry may overeat. Later, this action may make the person angrier. Other times, a person may blame another for becoming angry.

When someone is angry, they may direct anger against people who have nothing to do with the situation. Instead of confronting the person with whom they are angry, the angered person may lash out at family members, friends, or others who might not even be aware of the situation. An angry person may also direct their anger toward their surroundings. Hitting or throwing objects is an example of this.

Anger arises from an *event*. The event itself does not cause anger; the event causes a person to *feel* a certain way, which leads to anger. The energy created from anger must be directed somewhere.

When we feel angry we exert energy either toward the problem, which is giving rise to the anger, or toward a person. We are dealing with our anger from a positive perspective when we focus our energy toward the problem that caused the anger.

An example would be with John who owns a ten year old Ford Taurus. The car begins to smoke and then dies as John pulls to the side of the road. He walks to a gas station as he calls the car a piece of junk. He blames Ford for the poor quality.

What caused John to get angry?

It was not the car; it's his response to the event that triggered the anger.

What feelings are the true sources of John's anger?

John *feels* threatened because now he has no transportation, he is embarrassed, and fearful. He now has to pay an expensive repair bill.

Where is John's angry energy being directed?

He is verbally blaming the car and the car's manufacturer.

Where should John's angry energy be directed?

John should focus on the car and make sure that there is routine maintenance completed on the car. John may need to purchase a new car if he wants the security he needs.

How to know if you have a problem with anger.

Several ministers have confessed to me that they have a problem with anger. Not managing anger can lead to many problems within us and in our relationships with others. Here are a few indicators concerning a problem with anger:

- When you get angry you do not get over it. You find yourself repeating the offense in your mind, even holding a grudge.
- You are cynical about yourself, others or the world around you. You may tease others with "velvet daggers" in some of your jokes, only to be surprised when others do not want to be around you.
- You feel powerless to make the changes in your life to reach goals. You feel like a victim much of the time.
- Maybe you are angry all of the time. You may be verbally, emotionally, or even physically abusive to others in personal and professional relationships.
- You may feel depressed for long periods of time. You don't express your anger openly but take it out on yourself, whether you realize it or not. This can lead to suicidal thoughts and behavior or perhaps major illness.
- You never get angry. You just don't have emotion. There are times you know you should get angry but the emotions just don't seem to come. Therefore, you never fully release your anger.

If you have decided that any of these examples apply to you, then you probably have suppressed anger, or even rage. You must learn to manage and release your anger properly.

The Five-Step Process in Managing Anger

To direct the anger in a proper way it must first be managed.

1. Feel the anger.

Anger is an emotion and emotions are meant to be felt. To manage our anger we must first be aware that we are getting angry.

Usually we wait until life grabs us by the collar or the throws us to the ground before we really start to face our feelings. Even then, we only face them until we can get moving again. Why is that? Perhaps it is because we have all been hurt, and we don't really want to face that. None of us had a perfect childhood. The rest of our lives have also had some rough spots, so we've been hurt some more.

Most of the time we just keep on going. If we don't know how to be alone with our feelings, we bury them until they get too difficult, then we are eventually forced to deal with them. As long as we are alive, our feelings will not die. Experience your feelings while they are fresh.

2. Allow time for feelings to pass.

Many times we act too quickly and lash out in the wrong direction. Normally we vent our anger on the wrong person. Before you lash out count backward from one hundred to fifty.

3. Search for causes of anger.
Sources of anger
> Fear
>
> Loss
>
> Frustration
>
> Invalidation
>
> Needs not met
>
> Wounded feelings
>
> Poor communication

Whenever you become angry, make sure you focus on the specific reason for that anger. Once you are focused, it will become easier to work on strategies that will eliminate the source of frustration. If you fear losing your job, work on strategies that will keep you from losing your job, or look for a new position.

Anger can be a magnifying glass on your relationships. It can point to where problems exist so you can address them.

An example would be when a wife gets upset and yells at her children because they track dirt on the carpet. The issue may be she feels frustrated because of the lack of respect for the time spent cleaning the carpet and house.

Another example is when a husband gets angry when his wife spends more money shopping than she promised. The real issue may be that he feels she acted in an untrustworthy manner. The issues must be discussed completely.

4. Allow yourself to grieve.
I suggest that you write down what happened in the offense. Now accept your pain — your sense of loss is

real; this person - your mate, boss, friend, parent, church, or maybe even yourself - did take something from you or deny you something. Don't minimize it. He or she did not treat you with respect. Say the words: "You hurt me!"

Many people refuse to grieve their losses. They stay stuck in denial. They try to spiritualize by saying, "I'm strong. I'll get over it." It's much easier to allow yourself to hurt for awhile. Some serious offenses or losses need to be grieved — the pain acknowledged and released little by little. Depending on the magnitude of the loss, it can take months.

5. Communicate your anger.

Talking things over can often be the best way to settle your problems. As you communicate your anger don't get personal. Do not resort to insults and name-calling. These methods only cause more anger. Don't avoid the issue by hiding what you truly believe. Be direct, be straightforward, but don't get physical or violent. Avoid hitting or pushing the person with whom you're angry. Don't throw or break objects either. Don't make accusations that you'll regret later. Listen carefully to what the other person has to say before you draw any conclusions. Most of all don't sulk in silence. That method won't do anything to help solve your problem.

Calm down before you discuss the issues. Shouting matches rarely lead to effective solutions. Understand your motives before you express your anger. Are you trying to defeat the person, or are you trying to solve the problem? If your motive is negative, the results are likely to be negative too.

Be assertive not aggressive. Assertive people express

themselves firmly and clearly without making insulting remarks. They understand the importance of negotiating and compromising to resolve differences.

Use "I messages."

When we communicate our anger properly, we give clear, simple "I messages."

"You messages" are most often attacks, criticisms, devaluation of the other person, labels, or ways of fixing blame.

"I messages" are honest, clear, confessional. "I messages" own my anger, my responsibility, my demands without placing blame. Note the contrast between "I messages" and "you messages."

I Messages	You Messages
I am angry.	You make me angry.
I want the freedom to say yes or no.	You're trying to run my life.
I don't like blaming or being blamed.	You blame everything on me.
I feel rejected.	You're judging me.

Seek help if you are having trouble communicating your anger in a constructive way or if you're getting angry too often. Talk with a friend about your problem and seek a counselor for help.

Remember that anger is okay, and it can even be a good thing. It's just a normal feeling that we all experience. We have positive and negative choices in each situation. Keeping the other person in mind, learning from our mistakes, and working to make positive choices will help anger work for us, not against us.

Anger toward God.

There are times when we feel anger toward God, as well as others. When we go through a forced termination there are times that we wonder what God had in mind to put us through the pain? I have come to discover that God is big enough to accept my anger. Jeremiah was able to face God honestly with his rage. Elijah openly expressed his weariness and discouragement. David felt a freedom to talk about his anger toward God. We have the freedom to come before God and express exactly how we feel. The truth is, God knows anyway so why not express it?

Forgiveness can replace anger

Sometimes we think forgiving is admitting we're wrong or admitting defeat, or saying everything was my fault. Forgiveness is not giving in and agreeing with those who have hurt us. Nor is forgiving giving them our complete trust or forgetting the offense. Forgetting is more a result of short memory or subconscious suppression, while forgiving is an act of the will.

Forgiveness is a new beginning, starting at the present moment, the present situation. You don't start where you wish you were but at the place *where* you are.

In the Greek language the word for forgiveness literally means, "to let go." To forgive is to let go of anger, resentment, and revenge.

True forgiveness is saying, "I don't completely understand you. I can't excuse what's happened, and I can't forget what you've done, but I am now releasing the anger, resentment and bitterness from my life."

In my situation, true forgiveness has taken several years. My life had been altered forever by being forced to terminate my position as Senior Pastor. The hurt was very deep and anger was a part of my thought process. I realized that I could not get well unless I was able to forgive. I could not find peace and happiness, and at the same time, hold on to the feelings of anger. For me, to forgive those that hurt my family and me so deeply was a decision that I consciously made. I did not believe that forgiveness would magically happen one day. I made a conscious, intentional, and deliberate decision to forgive.

I found that forgiveness was not automatic or a one time act. Every day I had to make a conscious decision about how I was going to act and think and react in terms of those who I felt had wronged me. But, I found that each time I consciously forgave, it became easier to do so.

Following my forced termination, my wife and I spent over two years in Christian therapy. Our counselor taught us that anger is a feeling and forgiveness is a mental decision on which you act. When you begin to understand the other person, you will feel less angry. You can then decide to forgive. Forgiveness is a statement of intent, and it is a process.

For forgiveness to be real, you have to see the other person as a human being, not with malice or forethought, nor with the intent to harm. Once we see others as humans who are trying to make it in life, but who are hurting us in spite of what their intent may be, we are then able to accept and forgive.

I have found out that most of the time, the people who have harmed you are not even around to see your anger and resentment. I now realize that as long as I am angry with someone and have hostile feeling for him or her, that person has gained control over me. Once I grant them that power, I have given them the privilege to control my emotions.

More importantly, by hating or being angry, you are robbing yourself of energy because hostility is a tremendous waste of energy. This kind of energy is being wasted on a person who has long since forgotten the difficulty and has moved on to other things in life.

As you forgive, energy is now being freed to look at the future again, focusing on your positive traits that can be used to be of service in another place.

I have found it helpful to remember that as imperfect as I am and as many times that I have failed others, God continues to accept and love me while He continues to expect the best of me. I am convinced that God expects this kind of love out of us as we deal with others. We are not to be a "doormat," to those around us, but to love those around us as God loves us.

To forgive someone does not mean you no longer remember the difficulty. Something resulting in so much pain is not likely to be forgotten. I've learned that as you get on with life, your energies are invested in new accomplishments. As you do so, and as some successes come, the obsession of the forced termination melts away.

Even though you have been grievously wronged and the pain still rips through your spirit, you can rid yourself of anger and be a forgiving person. But you must give yourself time to work through the process.

CHAPTER ELEVEN

The Pastor's Family

A forced resignation affects the pastor, of course, but it also takes a heavy toll on the pastor's family. The need to find another church position or career creates a great deal of personal upheaval. Three-fourths of pastoral families surveyed by *Your Church* had to move to a new residence. Two-thirds reported that their children had to change schools. And nearly two-thirds of pastors' spouses had to change jobs.

In addition to the geographical and career changes, internal turmoil also makes an impact. Nearly six out of ten experienced a drop in their confidence as a leader. Most pastors report a heavy emotional toll on their spouse, and six out of ten say their family's ability to trust church leadership was undermined. On top of this, a surprising one in ten pastors experienced a major illness within twelve months of being forced out.

I have asked my wonderful wife of twenty-four years to share her insights about how the forced termination has affected our family. She has loved me, cared for me, given me wise council, and most of all, forgiven me and stayed with me through the most trying times of my life.

Marty's Insight

I used to tease that my husband Jeff had two speeds, fast and faster. However, it was not a joke. He was a full-fledged type A personality. He could not slow down nor could he let there be any loose ends concerning anything. He would work at least 70 hours a week at church and then an additional 15-20 hours at home on church re-lated work. I think for the first part of his ministry he was actually energized by this. Being a pastor was a joy for him. The first full time church we served in for three years was a new experience for us right out of seminary. The second church we served in for six years still feels like it should be home. Then there was the third church. That is where the burnout occurred resulting in forced termination.

Sometimes you look back and ask yourself, "Is this really what God had in mind for us here?" You start sec-ond-guessing yourself about hearing from God accurately. However, I have to acknowledge that there are numerous variables that are orchestrated by others, who have their own agendas that play into how your life evolves.

Things started out strained for us financially going to this new pastorate. We hadn't been able to sell our pre-vious home because the bottom had dropped out of the real estate market. So we had a house payment plus a rental payment for thirteen months. When we finally got the one and only contract for the house, we had to sell it at a loss. We had to take out a loan to pay the difference. I ended up working two and one half years to pay the loan off on that loss. When church members asked us to do things that would cost money we kindly declined without whining about our financial state. However, I'm sure those church members assumed we didn't want to be sociable, which was not the case. We just didn't have the money.

The first year my children were so unhappy that every night during our bedtime prayers they would cry and beg to go back "home" to our former pastorate. It was very hard for me to keep a positive attitude because I was feeling homesick myself. It was becoming more apparent to me that the church contained several cliques and I was not fitting into the "in" crowd. The church members were discovering that I am not an extrovert, therefore that means you are unfriendly. There were several comments made concerning that assumption which hurt me deeply. I certainly didn't expect every church member to be the life of the party, but I guess as my role as the "pastor's wife" I was supposed to be. Perhaps just using the gifts God had given me wasn't enough. I certainly know that our church contained some very wonderful people and I came to love them dearly. But even they could probably rattle off names of the "in" crowd. It saddens me to know that if I felt this excluded then others certainly did as well; not exactly what a church is supposed to be.

The first three years at this church were tolerable. Jeff was working extremely hard but the honeymoon was definitely over. As more time passed criticism was being given more often. Jeff received nasty notes from church members, of course always unsigned . . . how brave. He was trying to move the church to a progressive future. Of course, the usual suspects objected. There was one couple who was extremely hateful toward us. We invited them into our home for dinner to talk about their feelings and about the church's future. A few weeks later they asked

Jeff to come to their home. They decided they needed to let him know what a terrible pastor and person he was. And, "This was their church before he came and it would be their church after he was gone," they said. Funny, I was under the impression it was God's. I thought they made a sad pair. They obviously were just unhappy people to begin with. I've often wondered how many blessings they missed because they had closed their spirits.

A few more months passed and then there was a problem with a staff member who wanted to start his own church but take church members to do it with. That was a complicated mess. It was apparent that someone else was manipulating him and he just couldn't see it. Even after he left I think he came to realize on his own that he had made a mistake. He soon left the state to serve out west in another church position. Our family still loves his family and wishes him well even though at the time we were hurt by his actions.

Besides the constant gripes and complaints and the stress of this particular pastorate there was an event that we considered to be a real telling point of the church leadership's spiritual level. I won't go into detail but it boiled down to whether the leadership was going to allow the pastor to exercise biblical authority and to back him in what was right. The answer was no. I remember when Jeff came home from that meeting he was so discouraged. At the time I thought we should have looked for another church to serve in. Jeff did not agree. His heart was to stay because he thought he would need to be there for church members who might have a hard time with the fact that a staff member left the church and took other people with him. The church didn't bat an

eye. It was as if that particula*
to the next event. This is when *
Jeff. I encouraged him to get counse*
talks were no longer working. He had *
Instead he threw himself into a project, *
degree.

Jeff, I believe, was in search of finding *
where his talent would be appreciated. There*
much hurt inside of him because it seemed that with *
people no matter what you did, it wasn't good enoug*
When we were called to this church we were led to believe by the search committee that this church was ready
to "stop playing church" and be proactive in their world.
For the majority, that was not true. When Jeff tried to
exercise his leadership skills that he does possess in that
very area, opposition was hitting him over and over.
Sometimes you get tired of hitting your head against a
brick wall. You start thinking, "What is the use."

Jeff threw himself into earning a new degree. The
things that used to ignite his spirit were not allowed oxy-
gen so they could not breathe. This was a man who was
a soul winner, a champion for God. He had definitely
lost his passion for ministry. I know why. When a person
feels strongly God leading him to accomplish certain
tasks and there is a stronghold in the church that will
not let him do so; the joy is lost in the task. It has now
become a burden. That was a sad conclusion for me to
come to.

Jeff lost his focus and started making some poor decisions personally and professionally. The stress had become so great that at times he was hard to live with because he had become so unhappy. For him hard work

ξ things. So he in-
ed. He had become
rained. He was not

nd this is my opin-
lthy church. That
. The church staff
ff was interested
g secret meetings
onnel committee
not to have any

event was over. Now on
saw a real change in
ing because my pep
een beaten down.
etting another
omething
was so
hese
h.

.... staff by the chairman of dea-
cons and the chairman of the personnel. This never made
any sense to me. How are things to get resolved between
hurt parties if no one is talking to each other? Regardless it was decided that a mediator from our denomination would come in to help the church with the conflict.
The staff agreed that they would follow the mediator's
advice. After his interviews with the staff and Jeff and
me, the mediator concluded that Jeff should stay as the
pastor. Even though the staff agreed to follow his find-
ings they reneged and insisted that Jeff resign. So there
you have it. Everyone is allowed forgiveness but the pastor. He cannot be the one thing he is, that is human. Jeff
met with the leadership of the church and everyone got to
take his or her pot shots at him. From his account and
from another individual who was there, I was told that
they were very cruel. I was not allowed to attend this meeting, however the church secretaries were able to attend.

I don't know how Jeff was even physically able to
stand in front of this group. We hadn't slept or eaten in
days and he cannot afford to do this since he is hypogly-

cemic. I could barely function. He was in worse shape than I was. When he told me he was going to have to resign or face the threat of being fired I physically got sick and threw up. The day we decided to resign rather than to fight and possibly cause a church split was my son's seventeenth birthday. What a way to remember his birthday. We tried to celebrate a few days later, but he wasn't really up for it. I've been sad about that.

The feeling of total rejection cannot be captured in words. We were devastated. I looked so bad because I hadn't slept for so long. The night Jeff was to resign the Lord just gave me a calming spirit to help me be strong for my husband and children. It definitely was not under my own power. When we arrived it was like I was walking in a dream going through some strange motions. We entered the sanctuary and everyone was silent. It startled our daughter who was not prepared for such a reaction. Every eye was on us. Secretly I wondered if they didn't have a few rocks hidden somewhere in case they felt like they needed to stone us too. I actually felt like we were hated.

Jeff resigned with as much dignity as possible. Somehow we were able to get to our feet and leave the sanctuary. The church stood and gave us a standing ovation. It made no sense at all to me. When we left I fell apart. I thanked the personnel chairman for loving us. Now that I look back I find myself believing that it didn't have anything to do with love. We were just an inconvenient mess that needed to be tidied up and shipped out. That was his job.

When we got home we did feel a sense of relief that the resignation was over. But we didn't have the answer to what to do next. The children had the rest of the sum-

mer to try to adjust until the school year started again. I think they thought it would be an easier adjustment than it turned out to be.

As parents you try to protect your children as much as you can. Before the resignation we shared with them most of what was going on, but we tried to protect them from some of the uglier things that occurred. They both still wanted to go to church because of the strong youth group and most of their friends were church members. I didn't think it was a good idea because I was afraid they would get hurt. We expressed our concern but did not stand in their way of attending. Our son is pretty quiet generally and has a very forgiving spirit. To the best of my knowledge he and his friends didn't discuss what happened to his dad. Our daughter felt like her friends would hang in there for her as they said they would. Later she discovered that was too much of a commitment for many of them. Soon she wasn't being included with her friends for many of the activities. This hurt her very much. She lost her support system.

I watched as our children were responding as the reality set in. They both became depressed and were placed on anti-depressants. They weren't going to be able to shrug it off. But Jeff and I were no different. We also went on anti-depressants. I don't know how anything got done around the house. I didn't want to eat. When mealtime came the kids would have to remind me to cook for them. The house didn't get cleaned. Fortunately the children were old enough to do their own laundry. I later learned that I was in a stage of grief. I could hardly function to do everyday tasks. Even with the anti-depressant I wasn't sleeping well. I couldn't stop crying. Just when I would think that it wasn't possible to shed another tear, I would be in tears again. For months our whole family went to counseling to work through the grief and anger process.

We didn't move from the community. First of all our son would be attending his senior year of high school. These were kids he had gone to school with since fourth grade. Secondly, we didn't even know where to go. We felt stuck. It was hard knowing the chance was pretty good that you would run into a church member somewhere. After we finally moved from the community it helped the healing process speed up. If I had known how helpful it was going to be, I would have moved sooner.

Through the years in the pastorate, as every pastor and wife knows, you put up with the intrusion into your personal life. I guess since members contribute to the offering and they know a part of that offering goes toward your salary they feel that it gives them ownership in a sense. We've had comments ranging from the cars we drive, to the house we live in, to how to discipline our children, to the clothes we wear, to how long or short your hair is, to how long or short your skirt is, to whether you should teach a class or not, give a baby shower, attend a funeral, show up at the hospital at a certain time, to how well your children perform in school, to what movies you see, who your friends are, to where you take your vacation ...etc.; believe me the list is endless. These comments are not fun. I'm sure the giver of the unasked advice is sure that they know best but they themselves would be highly offended if the pastor or pastor's wife returned the favor and doled out their own advise to them. Usually I just smiled, said nothing and did what I felt was best and refrained from saying, "Buzz off!"

What a forced termination does to the intrusion of your life is a totally different matter. The pastor's role is not "a job." It is the life of the family. Since you and your family are there every time the door opens, it is your social life. It is where you meet and make friends. I know everyone says you should have friends outside the church but you just don't have the extra time. It is where you recreate, whether its the children having physical activities in their age groups or going to decorate the church for Christmas. If your family enjoys music, it's where you go to use your talents. It's where you can share with other believer's in the study of God's word in Sunday School. It's where you commune with God. It's your place of worship. But no longer, because those things have been taken from you as well. That's another form of grief you go through. The forced termination causes a total upheaval in your life. The church can write off the termination as just another chapter in the life of the church and forget about it. Unfortunately for the pastor and family their pain can't just be written down in the church minutes somewhere. They carry their pain in the form of emotional scars.

The hardest thing is watching your children suffer from the pain of what has happened. I would think that it affects all ministers' children no matter what their ages. The scariest thought for me is, "Will my children blame God and turn away from him completely?" Many pastor's children do turn away from God just from having grown up in a minister's home. I think churches would like to blame that totally on the parents but I feel that the churches probably have as much culpability. Many times the minister's children get to see hypocritical Christians who are very unchristian toward their parents. They get to see first hand the pain their parents suffer. Sometimes they determine they want to have nothing to do with God if this is how Christians act.

At this point I have hope for our son. He is now nineteen soon to be twenty and is doing some evaluating of his personal life. It's a hard time in his life. He has moved away from home to another state. That took courage. He is growing into young adulthood. Lately we've been talking about not neglecting his spiritual life. He had not been attending church but has recently started attending a church of our former denomination. I continue to pray that he will find a church committed to doing God's will.

Our daughter struggled after we moved from our former community. I felt she was like a ship lost at sea. She had lost her bearings. She did not want to go to school in the new community. We allowed her to get her GED. She was still on the anti-depressants. Because of loneliness and trying to find someone to share her pain she reached out to someone who took complete advantage of her vulnerability. Trusting him was not a wise decision. She got pregnant. When she told the young man, he wanted her to get an abortion. She refused. He immediately abandoned her. I think she is still working through some unresolved anger toward him. On July 18, 1999 God sent our grandson Jeremiah, five weeks early. He was in ICU for eleven days. He is healthy now and a joy to our lives. Unfortunately, our daughter is having to learn the consequences of being a teenage mother. Her goal is to go to college part time to earn a degree in mu-

sic. She has started going to church on a more regular basis with us. I'm starting to see her heart soften up to the things of God again. That is an encouragement to me. However, she still has some unresolved anger to deal with. I think in time she will.

One of the questions I've asked myself is, "How are we going to rebuild." I soon discovered I wasn't going to rebuild anything. It's been almost three years since we left the church and I'm still not sure of what direction God wants us to go. I do know that we have food, clothes, medical care, healthy children and Jeff has a job. So God is meeting our needs. Isn't that enough?

I do believe God has a plan. This book is a part of that plan. This book has been a long time in the writing. Because you can't write about dealing with anger or for-giveness until you have dealt with it. We have. Sometimes something triggers a memory of the past occurrence and once again we make the choice to forgive. I applaud Jeff for having the courage to write about a topic that is a tragedy for every ministerial family who goes through a forced termination. The church needs to open its eyes and take a hard look at itself. We like to condemn Old Testa-ment Israel for stoning it's prophets but is the modern church any less guilty?

How do the families deal with the forced termination? Look to God for healing. Decide you don't want to live with the pain that the anger causes any longer and make a choice to forgive. Ask the Holy Spirit to show you the error in your own life and to seek his forgiveness. Don't be ashamed to temporarily rely on medication prescribed by a doctor and to see a Christian counselor. Sometimes the medication is what helps to balance out the emotions so you can start thinking clearly to lead you to the path of healing God has for you.

I am grateful to once again see the spark come back into my husband. He's extremely talented and I feel sorrow for our last church that would not take advantage of the gift God had placed there in Jeff. This I do know, God will use Jeff to minister to others. In exactly what way we do not know yet, but we are open and willing.

Adam's Perspective (age 19)

"Fast and faster," is the statement my mother would joke around with when she talked about my dad's work habits. This was very true. Also true, is the statement, "busy and busier". At times growing up, I would ask my father to play catch, or any other activity that fathers and sons always do, and the answer was always, "maybe later son". When we moved to our third church, that response was becoming more and more of an answer of my question, "Dad, do you want to ...?"

Growing up as a pastor's kid, commonly referred to as a, "P.K.," people watch and scrutinize you for everything you do. I remember when groups of my peers would be acting up, I would be called aside, and told, "You especially cannot act like this, because you are the pastor's kid." As if I had a different level of morals and values I should have to live by. We are all human, and by being human we are all sinners. Pastors and their children sin just like everyone else; but for some reason everyone in the church feels like a pastor and his family are more wrong than everyone else when they sin. A sin is a sin, something that we do wrong that hurts God. And by me committing a sin, I am somehow hurting God more? That is a lot of pressure to put on a kid.

As I was getting older, and maturing, both mentally and spiritually, my parents were gradually sharing more with me about what was going on in the church. I began to see my mother and father getting noticeably saddened, and frustrated with every complaint. Everyone has to complain about something in the church. I think that churches these days have gone so far away from what Jesus originally taught us; just to simply "Love one another." Well, all of that love should start with your leaders. They should love, and in return be given back love. Well, as time went on, this was totally the opposite. It seemed like every time my father wanted to change things to where the church could glorify God more, the more complaints came in. At first they were simple complaints, and they just moved to worse and worse, and became ugly and uglier. At times as a young adolescent, I would just think to myself, "How do these people call themselves Christians?"

I myself have struggled with my spirituality. Kind of like a roller coaster. Sometimes I would be on fire for God, and other times I'd be lukewarm, the worst of all according to God. I never did anything horrible, in the world's eyes, but I know I was hurting God. There were times, now that I look back at them, when I was very strong spiritually. I'd always be willing to help people with their struggles in their faith, and usually God would help me help them ... and then ... it all came crashing down. First with the rumors, and then with the plotting against my father, and finally ended in resignation.

Right after his resignation, I didn't know what to think, or how to feel. I didn't know who was my friend, and who was my foe. I was very confused, and felt very belittled by the entire situation. I didn't know whether I should continue to be friends with some of my friends, because of what I had heard of what their families had said about, or done to my father. I decided that since I hadn't seen or heard anything first hand, that I shouldn't change my life or my friends. I kept going the same way I was, attending my youth group and going places with my friends. I think some of the most trying times for me were being in a friend's house with his family, the family who I had heard from my parents, as saying horrid things about my father. But I am a very forgiving person, as I feel I should be, and never once stared them down, or was disgusted by them. But it still hurt inside.

Throughout all of this confusion brought on depression. It was inevitable for me. I felt like I had to hide all of my feelings and hide my tears. I sat there and watched every single one of my family members crying, EVERY DAY! I couldn't cry. I couldn't be sad ... then what hope would there be? I had to give my family some hope! So I worked hard my senior year of high school. Going to a school I really didn't want to be at. I tried to do the best I could, even with the depression sinking farther in.

After the counseling and medication, I began to get better. I think our move away helped too. I started college, but I really didn't want to go. I didn't feel I was ready for it yet. Just as I was getting ready to tell my parents this, my sister got pregnant. This was a trying time for me and my family. I never thought of the possibility of my sister being pregnant. It was a shock to me, but I knew that we could get through it.

I didn't want to be in college, but now I felt like I had

no choice. I had to give my parents some hope ... again. So I did my very best in college, just to try to bring some satisfaction to their lives.

After one semester of college, I decided that I needed a change, a move. So I moved to the West Coast. I think the move has overall been good for me. There is more opportunity where I am now for the career I want to pursue. I have a great job that I am very happy with, and soon I hope to be going back to school again. I miss my parents, my sister, and my new baby nephew, but I know they will always be here for me and support me in whatever I do. Spiritually ... I have recently been going to a church. That is very hard for me after seeing everything I've seen, especially the scheming against leadership. I pray that this church will work out for me, and guide me back on the spiritual path I was once on. For all the P.K.'s out there, I know it's a hard long road to travel, but if you keep God as your focus, you will prevail.

Katie's Perspective (age 17)

The night my dad told our family that he was going to resign as pastor was the first time I ever saw him cry. Of course, the news took me by surprise and I began to cry as well. That night my life began to change drastically. I was a freshman in high school and my life as I knew it was great. Every weekend I had places to go and friends to see, I felt accepted.

School was a time that I looked forward to and my grades were good. I also looked forward to church attendance on Sunday's and Wednesday night. My spiritual life was better than it had ever been. But everything changed slowly but drastically.

The evening my dad resigned we were ushered in the church lounge. I remember thinking it was kind of odd that were kept away from the people. After prayer we left the lounge to enter the sanctuary. As the door opened I told myself that I would keep it together. When we entered the sanctuary the room became silent and I could hear my heart beat in my head. All eyes were on us. I felt as if we were about to get executed, or worse. I was thinking, why did I have to sit across from the youth section. I could see all of my friends faces, I was hoping they could not see me cry.

Following my dad's resignation we stood as a family and walked out of the church. When we arrived at home I went to my room and cried the tears that were left.

For a short time my brother and I attended church, but now realize it was a big mistake. We did quit a few weeks later. Things were so different, especially with my friends.

When school began I was alone, except for a few friends. I hated school. I did not want to get out of bed and would think of every possible excuse to miss school. When I did attend I would just sleep through my classes. All I wanted to do was to sleep.

I went through months of counseling and was on antidepressants, which helped some. By the end of the school year I was ready to get out of that town.

When we moved things did get better. We had a difficult time finding a church home, especially me. I never wanted to go to church. When I did all I could think about was how much I did not want to be there.

I thought things would get better as I entered a new school system, but they did not. I remember one morning as I arrived at school I couldn't take it, so I walked right back out. I could not make friends because I had trouble trusting people who said they wanted to be my friend.

While looking for a friend I found someone with entirely different intentions. I thought he was someone I could share my feelings with. I confided in him and explained what my family had been through. I soon found myself pregnant. When I told him, that was the last time I heard from my "friend."

In spite of all that has happened, I am now the happiest that I have been in a long time. I have my family and my beautiful baby boy, Jeremiah. I'm starting college soon and I am working part-time with my dad as my mom takes care of Jeremiah. We as a family attend a church that I am starting to get used to. I'm slowly learning how to trust again. I have grown up much quicker than I needed to. I know now that I can handle the difficulties that we face in life.

The forced termination has had a difficult impact on my family. We have had to regroup as we continue to work through many emotions. We have learned that tragedy will make you bitter or better. There were many times that the bitterness came out, even toward each other. In time, each of us have chosen not to be bitter, but to allow the forced termination to make us better. Our relationships are stronger and we enjoy each other on a daily basis.

Make Your Marriage a High Priority

When a pastor experiences forced termination it affects every core of his being and all of his relationships.

If the marriage of the minister and his wife is not strong, the relationship may be in danger following the forced resignation. A pastor must continue to work on the marriage and focus on the spiritual side of the union. God has placed you together and will give you the strength to make it through any predicament that you face.

The times our relationship was really strained was when both of us hit the bottom at the same time. There were times that the wounds were so deep that we could not even talk because we would get emotional.

I suggest that you go to a good Christian marriage counselor to help you sort through the feelings that you experience following a forced termination. You need a good counselor for the same reason you need a good surgeon when you have appendicitis.

Marty and I agree that our relationship has improved as we have worked through this crisis. We now are totally honest about our fears, our aspirations, and especially our feelings. We have learned to communicate clearly with each other and spend a great amount of time together.

Help Your Children Deal with a Forced Termination

One of the problems faced by a minister's grieving child is how he will handle strong feelings. One of the more predominant feelings associated with the forced resignation or dismissal of a child's father is anger. Even if your child has been taught to identify and express his feelings in ways that are neither harmful to himself or others, he may have a hard time unloading his anger. The children of terminated ministers often feel the brunt of a stigma attached to the father's job loss. In many cases, instead of being able to turn to the church as a source of help, many children feel rejected and alienated. The people who he turned to for help suddenly appear to be opponents. Anger, therefore, is easily coupled with the feelings of estrangement. Separation and loneliness are big factors to these children, and it can be even more threatening because their father is a minister. Minister's lives are usually meshed in the churches they serve.

After my interviews with several pastors who were forced to terminated I heard over and over again that one of the worst things about forced termination is that the children suffer terribly when they attend school. Children who listen to what their parents say at home say terrible abusive things. Some (minister's children) never get over it and never relate to a church again.

Here are a few suggestions on what you can do to help your children through the family crisis of a forced termination:

- *Assist your children in interpreting what has happened.* Many times a minister's reaction is bitterness and unforgiveness. If we allow this to continue to take place not only will the minister be tormented, but his children may remain in torment long after his own hostility has been resolved. Therefore, as you interpret what has happened, do it in the context of faith. Our faith does not despair in difficulty. Our life in God is bigger than a single church. If you are wrong in certain areas confess that before your family and ask their forgiveness.
- *Allow your children their feelings.* Denying feelings doesn't erase them. Instead they should be recognized and expressed. There is no comfort for those

who do not grieve. I made the mistake of allowing my son to hold on to his feelings. He was fearful that if he expressed his hurt it would create even more hurt for my wife and me. It was over two years following the forced termination that he was able to open up and talk to me about his feelings.

- *Locate a reliable Christian counselor.* A good Christian counselor can help the grief process in a tremendous way. My entire family went to counseling, as they needed someone to talk to about their feelings.
- *Locate a trusted pastor to allow you and your family to deal with your grief.* Even ministers and their families need pastoral care. Good pastoral care will assist the terminated minister, his wife, and their children to work through their grief.
- *Do what you can to preserve their normal family life.* The children have to face some difficult changes when their father is terminated. Parents are wise to keep those changes to a minimum. We stayed one year in the community following our forced termination so our son could graduate from high school. Later, he revealed to us that even though it was a difficult year, it would have been even more complicated if we had moved his senior year. Our daughter, on the other hand, wished that we would have moved sooner. My suggestion is to *try* to keep the changes to a minimum.

How Churches Can Help Children

So far I have given advice on how the terminated minister can help his children deal with the difficulty that surrounds a forced termination. What can churches do to help the children. I am convinced that the church that dismisses a minister does have a responsibility toward his children. Jesus spoke some strong words of warning when he said: *And if anyone causes one of these little ones who believe in me to sin, it would be better for him to be thrown into the sea with a large millstone tied around his neck. (Mark 9:42).* Regardless of the mistakes a pastor may make, the church should do all it can to avoid bringing harm to his children. It is normally not the children's fault that their father is dismissed from the church.

The church may find that they are in a quandary. How can a church force a pastor to resign, and at the same time bring the least amount of harm to his children? In reality, the children will experience hurt. Hurt is inseparable from forced termination. A church can help the children by giving at least, some short term financial assistance for the family. If the minister has been living in a church-owned home, the church should consider allowing him to remain there for a designated amount of time. That will take some of the pressure off of the entire family. They will not have to hurry to find housing.

It may feel awkward, but the church leadership needs to affirm the ministers' children, especially if they continue to attend the church. I suggest that you only try to affirm the children if you can be *genuine.* Several weeks after I was forced to resign, my fifteen year old daughter was trying to leave the church with a friend when one of the staff members stopped her and would not let her leave, and said "I love you and your family." My daughter felt the comment was phony because she knew the harmful things previously said about her father and mother by this person. She arrived home physically shaking and crying uncontrollably. That was the last time she attended the church. Please for the sake of the children be warm in your contacts.

If you are a pastor or church member that receives a terminated minister and his family into the fellowship of your church, you have received a family that has been hurt. The best chance for healing may come through your church. Many times we are broken by relationships, and we are likely to be healed by them as well. Keep in mind if the terminated minister and family choose to attend your church it is an expression of their continued faith in the church as God's way to redeem. Reach out and love them.

CHAPTER TWELVE

Where Do We Go From Here?

Recovery and Waiting on God

Forced Termination — the phrase evokes images of the end. Once fired up about pastoring, full of energy, dedicated, willing to give tremendously of themselves for others, now the pastor is without a church, and a job. When a pastor is forced to terminate, it is a time that can be used to focus on the spiritual side and wait on God.

Despite the disheartening picture painted in Isaiah 40, the prophet does hold out hope for those who were experiencing the difficulty brought on by the years of spiritual decline and failure in Israel. In verses 28-31 Isaiah presents the solution, which starts with the basic reminder:

> *"Do you not know?*
> *Have you not heard?*
> *The Lord is the everlasting God,*
> *the Creator of the ends of the earth.*
> *He will not grow tired or weary.*
> *And His understanding no one can fathom.*
> *He gives strength to the weary.*
> *and young men stumble and fall;*

but those who hope in the Lord
will renew their strength.
They will soar on wings like eagles;
they will run and not be weary,
they will walk and not be faint."

Recovery starts with a reminder.

Whatever problems the terminated pastor is facing; physical, emotional, mental, or spiritual, the prophet Isaiah points out to Israel ("Do you not know? Have you not heard?") that the wisdom necessary for solving their difficulty is already at hand.

Isaiah is doing what was needed for Israel then, which is the solution for the spiritual aspect of difficulty today. He is refocusing attention from the nation to God.

For me, hope came when I began to focus beyond my circumstances to the characteristics of the God I have served for years. As we put our complete trust in God, forced termination is a problem that can be solved.

Recovery is marked by a gift.

Isaiah also tells us that "God gives strength to the weary and increases the power of the weak." Just as salvation is a gift from God received by His grace through faith, and it is not by our own power (Ephesians 2:8-9), so the power and energy necessary to overcome a forced termination must be received as a gift from God.

Recovery is accomplished by waiting.

Finally, the prophet Isaiah reaches the heart of his solution for Israel. He shares that renewal of strength and hope is experienced by those who "hope in [wait upon] the Lord" (v.31). Today in our fast-paced society one of the most difficult aspects confronting us is waiting. Yet one of the most important biblical principles found throughout the Bible involves waiting. Waiting is an important component in our personal spiritual growth and spiritual development. It is designed by God to build in our lives a number of important traits.

Isaiah promises renewal of strength to those who wait upon and hope in the Lord. Like an old and battered car, the terminated and burned-out pastor's strength is depleted. He has been many miles and feels like he cannot continue on. The Lord's promise is that waiting on Him will bring renewal and strength. The pastor's old, tottering strength will be traded in for God's limitless energy. Physically, emotionally, mentally, and spiritually, he will become like new by waiting upon the Lord.

Don't despair, there is hope! There is a solution available to your difficult circumstances. By turning your attention away from your difficult circumstances and on to the everlasting God, you can find strength renewed. By waiting on God, you can find a consistent supply of wisdom and strength from God who is never weary, and who Himself will never experience a forced termination! God does know what the terminated pastor feels. Christ was rejected by His people, even suffering death on a cross.

Refueling to avoid another forced termination.

It is a terrible thing to be forced to leave a position in a church, but it is appalling to experience a forced termination a second time. A pastor or staff can use the time waiting upon God for the next assignment to refuel. Just like a car cannot run forever, a minister cannot continue to be effective without refueling. If we are to avoid burnout and the difficulty associated with burnout, we must find the resources to function. The following are intentional coping strategies. As we wait upon God for the next assignment we must allow Him to work on our hearts and lives.

Divine intervention

Certainly the most important intervention as we look deep within ourselves is divine intervention.

Meaningful prayer is vital as we wait upon God and listen to His still small voice. Find a private place. Daily get conscious of the presence of God. Read scripture aloud, talk to God and let Him know how you feel, and most of all — listen to what God says to you. Remind yourself of the promises of God and the comfort of His presence.

Look for the intervention of God in the expected and unexpected places. The worship experiences in church are one of the expected places. Following my forced termination I felt lost when it came to church attendance. My family and I attended several churches in our area but I did not feel a part of the church. I was used to being the spiritual leader, now I was sitting in the congregation. After several months we found a church that felt like home. The worship was so powerful that when we attended my wife and I stood in the presence of God and cried during the entire worship experience. God has used the church we are now a part of to heal our broken hearts and bring renewal to our souls.

Look for the intervention of God in the unexpected places. In the comment of your spouse, in the new place of work, in the response of your children. Look for the intervention of God in places where you would not ordinarily look.

Remind yourself of the promises of God. Read aloud the scriptures that show the promises of God. For example:

"Let not your hearts be troubled. Trust in God; trust also in me. In my Father's house are many rooms; if it were not so, I would have told you. I am going there to prepare a place for you." (John 14:1-2, NAS)

"For it is by grace you have been saved, through faith — and it is not from yourselves, it is the gift of God - not by works so that no one can boast. For we are God's workmanship, created in Christ Jesus to do good works, which God prepared in advance for us to do." (Eph. 2:8-10, NAS)

"Praise be to the God and Father of our Lord Jesus Christ! In his great mercy he has given us new birth into a living hope through the resurrection of Jesus Christ from the dead, and into an inheritance that can never perish, spoil or fade — kept in heaven for you." (1 Peter 1: 3-4)

Read these and other promises aloud. Keep yourself reminded of the promises of God. God is intervening in our lives to take care of our needs.

Confess your sins before God. As we allow God to work on our hearts we need to allow Him to do spiritual surgery. As God reveals areas that are not lining up with the scripture, we need to confess and allow God to perform surgery, cutting the sins from our lives.

It is safe to say, there are no innocent parties. I know it is possible there has been injustice. But you should assume that part of the fault lies in your own leadership and personal styles.

Your sin may be blatant. It is your sin — own it. The scriptures have taught us ways to deal with sin. Confess your sin to God. Repent of your sin. That means to stop doing it. Turn your life around and recommit your purpose. God does promise forgiveness, but He will not forgive if we do not repent.

Some ministers may be insulted by this kind of straight talk. But the truth is that there is no other way to deal with it. If it is sin, then it should be treated as sin.

The truth is that there are very few who were forced to terminate because of blatant or obvious sins. Most have been terminated or forced to terminate because of other difficulties. But, if the sin is there, confess it and repent.

As I look back over my forced termination, I do realize that I was in a deep state of burnout and in denial of that burnout. I made foolish judgement calls that created problems in my life and ministry. Even though I believe the church did not treat me fairly, I was part of the problem, not the solution. I have had to come before God and confess and repent of several sins that aided in my forced termination.

Self Intervention

As we allow God to heal our hearts, there is something we can do. We can be motivated with an earnest desire to effect change in our lives. We can visualize that desired result in our lives. We can simply relax and allow God to lead our lives. God has given each of us the ability to control the stresses that come our way.

Stress Management Begins in the Brain.

Stress tolerance begins in the brain. It is there that we must attack and change the conditioning process needed to manage stress. There are several basic methods of changing attitude that will lead to stress management.

- *Talk to yourself in a positive way.*

Normally when we find ourselves in a stressful situation we begin to focus on the negative and how it is effecting us. Whenever you find yourself in a stressful situation, take a minute to find something positive in the episode. While in traffic when people are cutting you off trying to reach their deadlines, say to yourself "I'm glad that I don't have to be in a hurry all the time, I can actually enjoy the drive."

- *Prepare yourself for upcoming stressful events.*

If you know that you will be walking into a stressful situation, prepare yourself mentally, then you will not be shocked by the event. For example, if you know you are going to have to talk to your chairman in leadership and he's the type of person that blows off steam, prepare yourself. Allow him to blow off his steam, but not let it effect you. If you go in with that attitude, the stress will be manageable.

- ***Don't dwell on the past.***
We cannot change what has happened in our lives, just the present, and maybe the future. Instead of worrying about what happened in the past, we can take a minute to use past experiences in a positive way. Maybe we made mistakes in the past. Learn from it and allow it to change your behavior.

- ***Visualize positive results.***
Normally when we are under stress we visualize all the negatives that could happen. Try taking a moment and think about a good result — expect success — the outcome of a stressful situation will come naturally.

- ***Be yourself.***
When we constantly try to please others and try to fit their mold, stress will be the outcome. In short, don't role-play. You will be more effective acting naturally than trying to fit a role. Place your confidence in yourself and your abilities. Consider your own limits as well as your strengths.
Pay attention to the way you are thinking and feeling in any given situation. It is important to learn what causes stress for you and your personal reaction to stress. Effective self-monitoring is your early warning system. It can alert you to the necessity of using other coping skills to prevent blowup.

- ***Accept what cannot be changed.***
We can accept what we cannot change by changing what we can. Make choices that are realistic, not out of reach.

• **Don't take on other people's stress.**
If you have the tendency to carry other people's problems around, you will feel the results of stress. There
are those who when stressed, love to give their stress to
anyone around them. Don't allow it to happen to you.
Yes, we need supportive relationships. We need those
with whom we can compare notes, blow off steam, and
get support for what we experience in life. But we must
be careful not to add to our stress by taking on the stress
of those around us.

Turning negative events into positive experiences
requires that we make a change in the way we think
and in our behavior. We must condition ourselves to cope
with stress through changes in our attitudes, which begins in the mind. Somewhere within all of us lies the
ability to bring out the best in ourselves. We have the
power to turn bad stress into good. We have the ability
to break the stress habit.

Learn Relaxation Techniques

For most people, relaxation is the best skill to learn
at the beginning of stress management. In the 1920s Dr.
Edmund Jacobson was beginning his career as a physician. He realized that, even when he was relaxed, his
muscles were still somewhat tense. He became aware
that this muscle tension might reflect the increasing pace
of life. Even in the 1920s almost every individual was
facing ever-growing demands that were almost unknown
to earlier generations. The average businessman was
striving to achieve more in hope of greater security. Busi-
nessmen fought off fatigue until they were exhausted.

The great stock market crash created anxieties simul-lar to unemployment and inflation. Dr. Jacobson realized that he, as well as his patients needed more than just encouragement to relax. Through his career, he developed a program for training people to relax their muscles thoroughly.

Over the years Jacobson and other scientists have refined progressive relaxation. It now offers a proven, systematic way to control muscle tension. More and more of the techniques are being established into physical fitness programs and exercise classes.

I teach the following relaxation techniques in my seminars and conferences as I teach how to prevent burnout.

How to do progressive relaxation

Begin learning relaxation by lying on a bed or reclining in a comfortable chair. Eventually you will be able to do these exercises while sitting or even walking.

Preparation

Spend some time getting as comfortable as you can. Loosen any clothes that are restricting. Slowly open your mouth and move your jaw from side to side. Let your mouth close, keeping your teeth slightly apart. Now, take a deep breath ... and slowly exhale.

Total body tension

Tense every muscle in your body. Tense the muscles in your jaws, eyes, arms, hands, chest, back, stomach, legs and feet. Feel the tension all over your body. Hold the tension, then silently say, relax and let go.

Close your eyes and take a deep breath, slowly breathe out and silently say, *relax and let go*. Repeat twice.

Head and face

As you keep your body relaxed, wrinkle your forehead. Try to feel the tension. Now, relax and let go. Try to feel the tension slipping out. Allow your forehead to grow smooth and take a deep breath. Hold it. When you breathe out silently say, relax and let go.

Open your mouth as wide as you can. Feel the tension in your jaw and chin. Hold the tension ... then let your mouth gently close. As you do silently say, relax and let go. Take a deep breath, hold it. As you exhale silently say, *relax and let go*. Repeat two times.

Hands

With hands at your sides, clench your fists as hard as you can. Keep them clenched for at least ten seconds. Release your hands and let your fingers slowly uncurl and go limp. Continue breathing deeply exhaling as you say silently, *relax and let go*. Repeat two times.

Arms

Raise your arms and clench your fists tightly for at least ten seconds. Allow your arms to fall limp by your sides. Your fingers should hang loosely. Now take a deep breath and exhale slowly as you say to yourself, *relax and let go*. Repeat two times.

Neck

Push your head back against a pillow or chair as hard as you can for ten seconds. Release your head and let it lie quiet and motionless. Continue your breathing as you say, *relax and let go*. Repeat this two times.

Shoulders

Shrug your shoulders up and try to touch your ears with your shoulders. Feel and hold the tension for ten seconds. Release and lower your shoulders slowly. Let them rest limply and heavily. Again, do the deep breathing while you say silently, *relax and let go*. Repeat two times.

Abdomen

Pull in your abdominal muscles as much as you can. Keep pulling them in for at least ten seconds. Slowly release your abdominal muscles. Continue your deep breathing as you say to yourself, *relax and let go*. Repeat two times.

Back

Keeping your face, neck, arms, and chest as relaxed as possible, arch your back up (or forward if you are sitting). Arch as if you had a pillow under the middle and lower part of your back. Notice the tension along both sides of your back. Keep your back arched for at least ten seconds. Now, relax and let go. Take a deep breath and hold it. As you exhale slowly quietly say, *relax and let go*. Repeat two times.

Hips, Legs, and Feet

Tighten your hips and legs by pressing down the heels of your feet into the surface they are resting on. Tighten these muscles. Keep the rest of your body as relaxed as you can and press your heels down. Now, hold the tension. Relax and let go. Take a deep breath and exhale slowly as you say quietly, *relax and let go*. Repeat two times.

Next, tighten your lower leg muscles. Now relax and let go. Take a deep breath and exhale slowly as you say quietly, *relax and let go*. Repeat two times.

Now, curl your toes downward. Curl them down and try to touch the bottom of your feet with your toes. Hold them and feel the tension. Relax and let go. Wiggle your toes gently as you let go of the tension. Take a deep breath and exhale slowly as you say, *relax and let go*. Repeat two times.

Spend a few more minutes relaxing. If during the day you find yourself getting upset about something, remember the relaxation you have just experienced. Before you get upset, take a deep breath, hold it, and as you breathe out silently say, *relax and let go*.

Actually with practice you will be able to use these techniques to relax whenever you begin to feel the stress of daily living.

Tension-relaxation is one of the best and most effective ways to learn relaxation because it conditions us to identify immediately between tensed and relaxed muscles. As a stress management tool, it's one of the best ways to train yourself to trigger the relaxation response whenever you feel stressed.

Develop a Network of Support

Ministers typically spend all of their lives meeting the needs of others. Especially after a forced termination a minister needs to develop a network of support. Here are some of the people that can help a pastor who has been depleted:

(1) Family

A wife or husband can be a best friend. Children can be people who can give support in time of need. The minister needs a supportive family. I feel very fortunate that my wife and children have supported me especially since I have tried to move beyond the forced termination and make a new life. As you read in chapter eleven my family suffered a great amount because of the difficulty we have experienced. We have stuck together and now our marriage is stronger than it has ever been. My relationship with my children has improved because I now have more time to spend with them. In fact, my priorities have changed where my family is above my career.

(2) Professional support

A minister needs a physician whom he trusts. A doctor who is a close friend can literally save the minister's life. I feel fortunate that God placed in my life a great medical doctor. Dr. Bill Whitley has been a trusted friend who has help keep me alive physically and emotionally. He genuinely cares about my well being and future.

God has placed a Christian counselor, Dr. Larry Cornine who has been a lifesaver for my family and me. Dr. Cornine has listened, prayed for, and given us wise Biblical council for three years. He has been a great influence to me as I have been writing this book.

(3) Intimate Friends

In the course of a lifetime, one develops only a very few really intimate friends. These are the people who give support no matter what. They do not judge. They do not disapprove. They are good listeners. They are trustworthy. I am fortunate that God has given me two such friends that have listened and supported me for over twenty-five years. One is in the ministry, Dr. Don Laughlin, the other owns a funeral home business, Spencer Hutson. These two men have been there for me. I can call them at a moment's notice and they would drop anything to listen and give comfort and support. Every minister needs intimate friends.

(4) Mentors

The mentors are those who can teach us by our trust in them. These are the persons whose opinions we respect so much that we turn to them in our difficult moments. These men and women are the specialists in our support system. We may not call on them often, but when we do we gain a great deal of strength.

Identity is more than the church

For men their identity is wrapped up in their profession. When men get together they talk about their jobs and positions, most are even known by what they do. I was a full-time pastor for over seventeen years. My success in the church and my acceptance of the people there defined a great deal of my self-esteem. Some of this perhaps comes from a misunderstanding, which is frequent among church people, about God's love. Although it may be at an unconscious level, many of us today still feel that we have to earn God's love. When I was forced to terminate, I felt that everything I had done was worthless. With all my efforts, I had failed. For a time, I felt like I was not a worthwhile individual.

Who am I today? With months of therapy and listening to God I am more confident than I have been in my life. Although I have not abandoned the ministry, I am pursuing my interests and talents in other areas. I am leading conferences on the subjects of burnout and stress. I am also working part-time for a company selling vacation ownership. I did not realize that I could be successful at anything but pastoring, but I can sell and am very successful as a closer. I have begun to see myself as a valuable person apart from the pastorate. I will do whatever God says. If he leads me to serve as a pastor again, I will go. My identity is not wrapped up in what I do, but who I am in Christ!

Career Satisfaction

As we accept ourselves as a unique, worthwhile individual it will lead to the understanding of our core identity. Once you know and accept that person that is deep within you, you are then free to develop a profession that is expressive of who you are as a person.

I believe part of the journey of life is about finding out who we are. One thing I want to emphasize about our own identity and our career choices is that God always wants the best for us. God will never call us to do anything that will conflict with our basic abilities. People who succeed in life are people who are in an environment that requires the skills they possess. When you are in a career that allows your strongest skills that relate to your personality, you will find success.

The best course of action is to find your God-given identity and be true to it. You will be happier, your spouse and children will be happier, and if you pastor again your church will be happier and respect you as a model.

Accepting a secular job is not defeat. You may be forced to become a temporary tentmaker. This does not signify defeat. This only means you have planned to fill the interim with meaning.

You may never serve as a pastor or on a church staff again. You can still find satisfaction in working a secular job, and receiving gratification as you serve in your church or start some type of ministry. There are an infinite number of variables in the workplace. To achieve career satisfaction, you need to figure out what your preferences are and then find a job that accommodates them. Some jobs provide warmth and stability; some are risky and challenging. Some are structured, some aren't. One job may require a lot of socializing, while others may require quiet concentration.

The secret of career satisfaction lies in doing what you enjoy most. A few lucky people discover this secret early in life, but most are caught in kind of a psychological wrestling match, torn between what we think we can do, what we (or others) feel we ought to do, and what we think we want to do. My advice? Concentrate instead on how God has wired you up, who you are, and the rest will fall into place.

By making a conscious effort to discover how God wired you up, you can learn how to focus your natural strengths and inclinations into a career you can love as long as you choose to work.

Each one of us has a distinct personality, like an innate blueprint that stays with us for the rest of our lives. We are born with a personality type, we go through life with that type, and when we die, it is with the same type. As you discover your personality type you will be able to find a career that you will enjoy.

As I worked on my Doctor of Ministry degree, my project dealt with matching the right personality type with the correct ministry position. For example, I suggest when you hire a Church Administrator you probably will need to allow God to lead you to a person that is an introvert with great sensing and thinking abilities. Most administrators work directly with church records, books, and spend much time alone.

I took what I learned from my project and applied it to myself as I began to look for secular employment. I am an extrovert who feels rewarded when a job is finished. I reach closure by making quick decisions. I found a job for a resort at an offsite location. Telemarketers brought in clients each evening to consider purchasing vacation ownership. I served as the podium speaker (extrovert), I moved quickly from salesman to sales manager and closer (quick sales). I completed several jobs an evening giving closure to my task.

I also started Barnes Institute where I am able to use my gifts and abilities as a teacher and speaker. I lead seminars on the subjects of burnout, stress management, time management, and matching your personality with your career. I truly feel satisfaction as I am able to be the person God has called me.

If God leads me to pastor again, I will not allow myself to be placed in a box by the expectations of a few people in the church. I will be me. The person God loves and cares about.

Epilogue

Today I am much wiser living through and gaining character from a forced termination. I have preached for years that going through a crisis will either make you "bitter or better." Believe me, the temptation to live a life of bitterness is an easy route to go following a forced termination. My family and I have chosen to follow the scripture especially as it relates to helping others through the same difficulty you have experienced.

My suggestion is that if and when you accept a position in another church, don't be naïve. I do believe that God leads us, but He also gives us minds to make good judgement calls. Know what you are getting into. It's all right, even a good thing to ask questions. Ask all the questions you need until you feel sure you understand the church that is considering you as their leader.

Discover who has the power to hire and fire in the church. For what reason could you be fired? How are performance reviews handled? Who gives them? When?

Study the church bylaws and minutes of business meetings. What does the church expect of the minister's spouse?

Be open and straightforward with the church concerning your expectations. Place in writing what your responsibilities will be and how those responsibilities will be reviewed. A written contract may seem too business-like in a spiritual institution, but it will clarify issues and be helpful to the minister and the church.

By all means, investigate the history of the church. Call former pastors and ask them how they were treated and how they were able to minister. Knock on doors of homes near the church and ask about the reputation of the church. Interview members that are not in key positions of leadership.

You can move ahead, ministering in another church, still believing in the God who calls you, but also moving forward gentle as a dove, but as wise as a serpent.

Burnout Barometer

The following test is one way to determine how prone you are to burnout. Following the test is a scoring key that will help you determine what stage of burnout you may be in.

	Seldom	Sometimes	Always
1. I feel angry at work.	1	2	3
2. I feel that my career is not moving forward.	1	2	3
3. I find myself thinking negative thoughts about work even at bedtime.	1	2	3
4. I wonder if I can make it through another day.	1	2	3
5. I feel tired and exhausted all of the time.	1	2	3
6. I call in sick frequently.	1	2	3
7. I find myself taking out my work frustrations at home.	1	2	3
8. I focus on what is bad at work.	1	2	3
9. I feel I must succeed all of the time.	1	2	3

10. I am spending less time with co-workers.	1	2	3
11. I am not as productive as I used to be.	1	2	3
12. My time at work is less organized.	1	2	3
13. I avoid contacts, even with friends.	1	2	3
14. My temper is shorter than ever before.	1	2	3
15. I feel that no one at work really cares.	1	2	3
16. It is impossible to complete what I'm assigned.	1	2	3
17. I am insensitive to my co-workers.	1	2	3
18. I feel powerless to make changes.	1	2	3
19. Work is boring.	1	2	3
20. I ask myself if my job is right for me.	1	2	3

Total points: _____

Scoring: **20-34** **No Burnout**
35-49 **Moderate Burnout (early warning signs)**
50-60 **Severe Burnout (need help and guidance)**

ORDER FORM

Please send _____ copies of

"To Fight or Not to Fight: Should a Pastor Resign Under Pressure Or Stay and Fight?"

Name _____

Address _____

City/State/Zip _____

Price	16.95 per book	_____
Sales Tax *(Kansas Residents)*	1.00 per book	_____
Shipping and Handling	3.00 per book	_____
Total		_____

☐ Check   ☐ Visa   ☐ MasterCard

Card No. _____ Exp. Date _____

Signature _____

Use this form or photocopy and mail to:

BARNES INSTITUTE
10308 Metcalf Ave. # 409
Overland Park, KS 66212-1800

ORDER FORM

Please send _____ copies of

"To Fight or Not to Fight: Should a Pastor Resign Under Pressure Or Stay and Fight?"

Name _____

Address _____

City/State/Zip _____

Price	16.95 per book	_____
Sales Tax *(Kansas Residents)*	1.00 per book	_____
Shipping and Handling	3.00 per book	_____
Total		_____

☐ Check   ☐ Visa   ☐ MasterCard

Card No. _____ Exp. Date _____

Signature _____

Use this form or photocopy and mail to:

BARNES INSTITUTE
10308 Metcalf Ave. # 409
Overland Park, KS 66212-1800